DEAL!

Discovery,

Engagement,

and

Leverage

for Professionals

Guiding Clients to
Good Decisions

DEAL!

Discovery, Engagement, and Leverage

for Professionals

Guiding Clients to Good Decisions

JEFF BELKORA

Guidesmith Press
San Francisco, CA

DEAL! Discovery, Engagement, and Leverage for Professionals
Copyright © by Jeff Belkora, 2015.
All rights reserved.
No part of this book may be reproduced in any form by any means without the express permission of the author. Email jeff@jeffbelkora.com to seek permissions; for information about bulk orders; and for all other author correspondence.

Published in the United States by Guidesmith Press

Print edition 1.41
Purchasing this print edition from Amazon qualifies the buyer for a discounted price on the latest 1.xx edition of the ebook, through Amazon's Matchbook program. In addition, all future 1.xx editions of the ebook are available to purchasers of any earlier ebook edition from Amazon. Contact Amazon customer service to request that the latest edition be added to your account. Updating your edition will overwrite any highlights or notations that you made on any prior edition of the ebook.

ISBN 978-0-9966577-1-6
Library of Congress Control Number: 2015914465

Please help *DEAL!* find its audience by posting a review on its Amazon page at http://amazon.com/dp/0996657711, also accessible via the shortcut www.jeffbelkora.com/dealbook.

Cover image used under license from Shutterstock.com

Disclaimer: This book contains examples that illustrate various tools and techniques of critical reflection. Some of these examples involve people making medical, financial, and other decisions. These examples do not constitute advice, and you should not rely on the information they contain when making your own decisions.

Contents

The map is not the territory.

Alfred Korzybski

About the Author	vii
Welcome	ix
Target Audience	xi
The Story Behind *DEAL!*	xvii
Section 1: *DEAL!* Ingredients	25
Chapter 1: Five Life Drivers	27
Chapter 2: Decision Quality	41
Chapter 3: Critical Reflection	61
Chapter 4: FAST Critical Reflection	83
Section 2: *DEAL!* Recipes	99
Chapter 5: Discovery	101
Chapter 6: Engagement	133
Chapter 7: Leverage	173
Chapter 8: Let's make a DEAL!	201
Executive Summary	213
Bibliography	221
Acknowledgments	231

About the Author

I hate quotations. Tell me what you know.

Emerson

Jeff Belkora, PhD is on a mission to help professionals guide clients to good decisions. Belkora is a faculty member at the University of California, San Francisco (UCSF) School of Medicine. There he founded and directs the Patient Support Corps, which serves patients and families navigating major medical decisions.

The US Agency for Healthcare Research and Quality selected Belkora's patient support program as one of the first 100 innovations profiled in the Innovations Exchange, giving the program's evidence base the highest possible rating ("strong"). Subsequently, the US Department of Health and Human Services featured this program in its 2010 National Healthcare Quality Report as a highlight in the area of patient and family engagement. The Mayo Clinic Center for Innovation also selected Belkora's program as a winner in a national contest recognizing innovators in health care.

Belkora also works with other organizations as a speaker, consultant, and trainer. He has published accounts of his work on discovery, engagement, and leverage in leading peer-reviewed journals ranging from the Journal of Clinical Oncology to the Journal of Wealth Management.

Belkora earned a Bachelor of Science degree in Applied Mathematics from Brown University; and from Stanford University, a Master's in Statistics and a PhD in Engineering. Prior to UCSF, he worked at Strategic Decisions Group and Outcome Software. Outside of work, Belkora enjoys time with his family and friends; plays soccer and basketball; and writes songs.

Welcome

Don't bore us; take us to the chorus.

Berry Gordy, Jr.

Thank you for supporting our common cause with your purchase of *DEAL!* We are now joined in a mission that matters to us both: guiding clients to good decisions. Our mission is vital because clients turn to a professional when they are at a significant crossroads or crisis representing danger or opportunity. The quality of their lives hangs in the balance.

My hope is that you and your clients will experience extraordinary returns on your investment when you use my tools for discovery, engagement, and leverage. I am happy to share these profound and powerful tools with you, based on over 20 years of research and practice. This has been my life's work and my labor of love. For maximum clarity, I suggest you consult the executive summary at the back of this book for a roadmap as you read. You can also download the summary at www.jeffbelkora.com/deal-executive-summary.

Please help other mission-driven, client-centered professionals find *DEAL!* by posting a review on its Amazon page at http://amazon.com/dp/0996657711, also accessible via the shortcut www.jeffbelkora.com/dealbook.

Please spread the word on social media using #thatdealbook.

If you would like me to speak, train, coach, or consult with you or your colleagues, or you would like to connect for other reasons, please email jeff@jeffbelkora.com. I'm also on Twitter @jeffbelkora, and on the web at www.jeffbelkora.com.

For occasional updates by email, and to register your copy of *DEAL!* for relevant offers (such as new editions), please join my distribution list at www.jeffbelkora.com/esubscribe.

Target Audience

All professions... are conspiracies against the laity... the military conspiracy, the legal conspiracy, the sacerdotal conspiracy, the pedagogic conspiracy, the royal and aristocratic conspiracy, the literary and artistic conspiracy, and the innumerable industrial, commercial, and financial conspiracies, from the trade unions to the great exchanges, which make up the huge conflict which we call society.
George Bernard Shaw, *The Doctor's Dilemma*

DEAL! is aimed at professionals: accountants, advisors, architects, bankers, brokers, doctors, lawyers, nurses, teachers, therapists and others with technical expertise who guide clients in crisis. You are my audience.

You should be angry when George Bernard Shaw accuses you of "conspiring against the laity." He charges you with guiding your clients to decisions that are good for you, not for them. Those are fighting words. I am here to help you fight these charges of professional-centered practice.

Specifically, this book presents a new DEAL for professionals: new heights of client-centered practice through better discovery, engagement, and leverage. My prescriptions for discovery and engagement will help you and your colleagues surface and attend to the true needs of your clients. You will guide clients to good decisions on their terms. My prescriptions regarding leverage will help you sustain the cost-effective delivery of such client-centered practices.

How does Shaw's conspiracy against the laity arise in the first place? You go through arduous training and licensing to become the professional of your dreams. Then you work incredibly hard, in an increasingly rigid regulatory environment that encroaches on your professional autonomy and flexibility.

I see up close how hard you work. Recently one of my physician colleagues was nominally on vacation. But her patients were not on vacation. So she checked her emails and jumped in to direct care, from far away, when a patient's trajectory took a turn for the worse. That's the norm among professionals. There is no such thing as taking a full break. You're always on duty, to some degree.

So you have no intention of conspiring against your clients! How dare Shaw suggest this! Yet along the way, you inevitably fall into a gap between professionals and clients, a gap known as the agency problem.

The agency problem simply states, from the client's point of view, that a professional acting on my behalf may not act in my interest.

Some degree of mission drift is inevitable between professionals and clients. Professionals cannot know client interests at all times. We clients are, after all, strangers even to ourselves.

However, professionals should always strive to be true fiduciaries, putting the client agenda ahead of their own, and guiding clients to good decisions on that basis. You can continuously improve in this quest. That is the essence of what I will call *professionalism*—the drive to guide clients to good decisions that advance their agenda, and the drive to continuously improve.

Against considerable odds, many of you are able to practice in this way as fiduciaries. For example, when I was considering LASIK eye surgery, I went to see Dr. Richard Abbott at the Beckman Vision Center at UCSF. People magazine had profiled Dr. Abbott as the rare LASIK eye surgeon who still wore glasses himself. And, true to form, after eliciting my goals and priorities, he counseled me against having surgery, given my condition.

Dr. Abbotts of the world, I salute you. I believe even you can benefit from this book because there is always room for improvement, and the highest achievers are always the most devoted to the pursuit of perfection.

Others among you may be in more dire straits, despairing of the environment in which you practice, and losing hope that you can be truly client-centered. You look around, including in the mirror, and you see professional-centered practice more than client-centered care.

What are the hallmarks of professional-centered practice? In the words of the Institute of Medicine, "Care is organized for the benefit of the professional and/or institution."

For example, in professional-centered encounters:

- The professional speaks more than the client.
- When the client does speak, the professional interrupts early and often.
- The professional uses jargon.
- The professional guides clients to decisions that may not serve the deeper client agenda.
- In fact, the professional-centered practitioner would prefer not to surface the deeper client agenda, because it is inconvenient and gets in the way of advancing the professional agenda.

In professional-centered delivery systems, the professional is expensive and fees increase every year. The professional fiercely defends against encroachment on professional turf by other providers. And in professional-centered delivery systems, the billing system works even when nothing else does.

In professional-centered politics, advocates lobby for doctors rather than patients; lawyers rather than laypeople; teachers rather than students.

I understand that professionals need to operate with a sustainable business model and in working conditions that allow them to serve client interests. I realize that revenue and pay and caseload and working hours are important issues for professionals.

In my view, however, the key to advancing client interests sustainably is to focus first on the client interests and second on engineering a service delivery model that efficiently supports such client-centered practice. This is what disruptive innovators are doing across the board.

In contrast, the professional system, by definition, has prioritized the institutionalization of its service delivery model, and is often focused on defending it rather than on truly advancing client interests. This is *professionalization* rather than *professionalism*.

If you are candid and self-aware, you will admit that this is one of the reasons, however implicit, that you became a professional: because of the legitimacy and security bestowed upon your career path by professionalization. Now, further down the road, you see that professionalization is a double-edged sword, and that your professional structures both serve and hinder client interests.

What I am saying is that *the long-term goal of a profession should be to put itself out of business.* Doctors should be working on preventive health so that the use of medical care decreases every year. Lawyers should be simplifying the legal system so that laypeople can navigate it alone. Teachers should be designing curricula that students can self-administer.

Paradoxically, as you put yourself out of business, new business structures will emerge, because there is always more value to add to people's lives if we can only adapt quickly enough.

Instead, as a class, professionals, whether inadvertently or intentionally, erect barriers to advancing client interests, rather than tear them down.

My methods for discovery, engagement, and leverage will help you tear down those barriers from the professional side, before laypeople lay waste to your profession from their side of the ramparts. I am here to help you in your quest to become or remain client-centered, and to resist becoming more professional-centered.

Reading this, you are probably beginning to wonder about my own self-serving motivations—and you should! I fully hope to profit from your purchase of this book, and my related speaking, training, and consulting services. But like you, like most professionals, my main motivation is pro-social and I hope to align my enlightened self-interest with my altruism.

I am writing this book because we, the people, need you, the professionals. We need professionals with deep technical expertise. We need your guidance. And we need you to be focused like a laser beam on serving our agenda. So I am writing to share certain lessons I have learned regarding how you can be even more focused on client interests.

Now, I fully appreciate that some of you may resist my diagnosis of the overarching problem. Perhaps I am casting the problem in overly grandiose terms: a conspiracy against the laity! Professionalization triumphing over professionalism!

Perhaps I am casting myself in too messianic a role: I can save you from professional-centeredness!

You may be right. In that case, you can read this book simply as a manifesto for continuous improvement. I believe you will find valuable tools and techniques for incremental improvement, and I hope that is sufficient reason to invest your money and time in this book, and in my other products and services.

Either way, I can help you in this quest for client-centeredness because I am an outsider working on the inside, a non-physician (systems engineer) working with health care professionals, a patient advocate running a patient support program in a large medical center. Because the dynamics are so similar across professions, I think you will find that the lessons I have learned are relevant to any professional practice.

I got my start in my primary field of patient advocacy as a graduate student, 24 years of age, volunteering in a resource center for women newly diagnosed with breast cancer. One of the other volunteers said to me, "Jeff, we don't know what to make of you. You have four strikes against you. You're young. You're male. You've never had breast cancer. And you're an engineer. And we can't agree on which is the worst thing!"

Well, twenty years down the road, I'm down to three strikes. And I hope that even after this inflammatory quotation from Shaw, and this prefatory polemic, my audience still includes the professionals listed alphabetically below. Am I missing any? You make for strange bedfellows when presented together in this way. But you share a common mission: guiding clients to good decisions.

- Advisors, agents, and architects
- Bankers and brokers
- Coaches, consultants, and counselors
- Doctors and designers
- Engineers and emergency responders
- Lawyers and librarians
- Managers and ministers
- Nurses and negotiators
- Salespeople and social workers
- Teachers and therapists

Welcome to the new DEAL!

Join the movement for continuous improvement!

Guide your clients to good decisions!

Read on!

The Story Behind *DEAL!*

You can't connect the dots looking forward. You can only connect them looking backwards.

Steve Jobs

Hello, my name is Jeff Belkora. I'll be your guide as we review some tools I have developed to help you and your clients navigate complex terrain. You can use these tools to navigate yourself or to guide others.

A little about my journey: I was born in Denver, CO and grew up in Geneva, Switzerland, where my parents worked for the United Nations, promoting international trade and economic development. At the age of 18, I came to the United States for college. I studied Applied Mathematics at Brown University, and then went on to Stanford University where I earned a Master's in Statistics, and a PhD in Engineering.

At a young age, I became fascinated by how people lead their lives and respond to problems and opportunities. For example, I was an avid reader of biographies and self-help books. Eventually, this passion led me to the study of leadership, teamwork, and decision making, which I see as the key artistic tools of personal and professional growth. I wrote my doctoral dissertation on decision making in medicine.

One of my PhD advisors was a surgeon, Dr. Laura Esserman. Laura is among the more client-centered professionals I have ever encountered. I attribute this to two influences in her life.

First, Laura's father runs a successful network of car dealerships that distinguish themselves based on customer service. Laura absorbed this ethos growing up. For example, Laura will not walk by a visitor wandering our hospital lobby without asking if they need directions or any assistance.

Another telling example: when our hospital purchased its first MRI machine, Laura had an MRI herself so she could personally experience what her patients would experience.

The second reason Laura is so client-centered is because she went to business school. Many of our most patient-centered physician leaders have business or public health degrees in addition to their advanced medical degrees. At UCSF, the clinicians who have most championed my work include Laura Esserman, MD MBA, Kevin Bozic, MD MBA (now at the University of Texas), and Peter Carroll, MD MPH. Those extra letters count for a lot. They may be neither necessary nor sufficient, but they indicate a great degree of cross-training in an otherwise highly specialized health care professional.

Back to my journey through graduate school. Because of my engineering background, Laura initially wanted me to develop quantitative models to teach patients about options and outcomes and help them choose the best treatment.

That's what systems engineers often do—we design systems and make trade-offs. Our bridges, space shuttles, computers, and semiconductors must weigh the advantages and disadvantages of different designs in terms of performance, cost, safety, aesthetics, and so forth. Similarly, patients and doctors must balance their desire to maximize length and quality of life against the risks of harms, complications, and side effects of different treatment options.

At first I agreed with Laura, and we did build some quantitative models together. However, after shadowing various doctors and their patients in the intensive care unit and cancer clinics, I realized that patients needed something much more basic and fundamental than quantitative models. Patients needed to activate their critical thinking about what treatments to take. Otherwise, as passive patients, they were at risk of having a doctor make decisions on their behalf that did not necessarily serve their interests. Doctors make different decisions than patients for many reasons, including a different worldview, as well as conflicts of interest.

For example, the very first patient whom I observed was coming to consult with Laura about treatment for breast cancer. Laura initially thought this patient would benefit from breast conservation: a lumpectomy, followed by six weeks of radiation.

After attending their meeting, I showed Laura my notes from my earlier interview with this patient. The patient had told me, "I want to take my mother, whose eyesight is failing, on a cruise—while she can still see."

This was an aha moment for Laura, and for me. Laura said, "She didn't tell me about her mother. This changes everything. If her goal is to get to that cruise as quickly as possible, I would recommend a mastectomy with delayed reconstruction."

Upon further deliberation, the patient agreed, and enjoyed the cruise with her mother before having a reconstruction upon her return. Laura had the good sense to adapt her recommendation upon realizing that she was initially viewing the situation differently than the patient. This difference in the worldviews of doctors and patients is one cause of the agency problem, where professionals acting on our behalf may not act in our interest.

As a result of this case, Laura said to me, "I think of myself as doing a good job of communicating with patients. But it would have been helpful to have your notes on the patient concerns before I conducted my consultation." So I developed a set of methods and tools to discover and document the patient agenda prior to medical visits, and focused my doctoral dissertation on this topic.

Everything I have done since then can be traced back to this period of immersion in the patient experience. Over a two year period, I accompanied over 200 patients to their meetings with surgeons and oncologists, helping them prepare questions beforehand; taking notes for them during their visits; and debriefing afterwards.

In the course of my research, I reviewed hundreds of hours of recordings and transcribed dozens of interviews and interactions. Transcribing conversations is the most effective way, in my view, to study communication. When you transcribe a conversation, you absorb the contents and patterns of communication through your fingertips, in slow motion.

Transcribing your own conversations can be incredibly painful. Donald Kennedy, President of Stanford when I was a graduate student there, used to say, "As an evolutionary biologist, I am here to tell you that the purpose of pain is to avoid the recurrence of stupidity." I emerged from my doctoral study as an expert on preventing the recurrence of my own stupidity in conversations. Overall, I developed deep expertise on the topics of critical reflection, communication, and decision making.

Upon graduating, I could not discern a career path as a patient advocate, so after completing my PhD, I started a software company with friends from graduate school. We built financial engineering software for large companies. I was in charge of technical sales, which means I accompanied our salespeople on visits to prospective customers. I learned a lot about software and the pharmaceutical, health care, banking, oil and gas, and other industries. I also learned about launching, financing, and growing new ventures.

Eventually, I realized that I wanted to get back to patient advocacy. I took some time off and, in dealing with a minor health issue of my own, came to realize I had assembled most of the ingredients for a comprehensive patient support program. Laura Esserman suggested I rejoin her at the University of California, San Francisco (UCSF), where she had moved and was leading the breast cancer clinic.

In another career changing aha moment, Laura provided a key missing link to my vision of a comprehensive program. She suggested that we could staff my patient support program with student interns as a low cost but highly effective labor force.

The Story Behind DEAL! (Belkora)

So I did rejoin Laura at UCSF, and have since directed a program that provides educational materials and health coaching services to patients, initially in breast cancer, and now in other life-threatening conditions as well. We inform and involve patients and families so they can make decisions that are right for their unique circumstances and priorities.

The basic problem we address is that too often people respond to a cancer or similar diagnosis with a fight, flight, or freeze reaction. This dynamic exacerbates the agency problem, where professionals acting on our behalf may not act in our interest.

The fight/flight/freeze reaction and agency problem create a severe risk of under-treatment or over-treatment in medicine. In other words, patients are at risk of getting too little or too much treatment relative to what they would prefer if fully informed. For example, elderly patients are at risk of being under-treated with hip or knee replacements, while being over-treated at the end of life, when they would prefer to die at home.

This dynamic also occurs outside of medicine: clients may be treated with too little or too much professional service, compared to what is appropriate given their condition and personal goals. For example, in financial services, under-treatment occurs when people struggle with issues that could easily be addressed by the right professional. Over-treatment means that someone is selling clients solutions they don't need.

Today, our patient support program at UCSF uses a leveraged workforce (student interns) to discover the patient agenda and engage in decision support. Hence the title of this book: Discovery, Engagement, and Leverage, or, to use its acronym, DEAL. DEAL helps our professional care teams focus like a laser beam on discovering the patient agenda and engaging in decision support to advance that agenda. My program helps patients obtain Goldilocks treatment—just right for their condition, personal goals, and priorities

Based on our experience, I've now trained hundreds of other patient advocates and health educators, ranging from surgeons and oncologists to nurses, social workers, psychologists, and student interns. These advocates have served thousands of patients making high stakes decisions about cancer and other life-threatening conditions at UCSF and other hospitals and clinics. The US Department of Health and Human Services, the Mayo Clinic Center for Innovation, and others have recognized my patient support program as a leading innovation with a strong evidence base.

My colleagues and I have grown this program and exported elements of our design to other organizations, including the Cancer Support Community, a nationwide network of resource centers that support patients and families dealing with cancer. I've founded the Patient Support Corps to further spread this model of discovery, engagement, and leverage in health care.

Outside of health care, I've advised and trained people in non-profit and for-profit organizations. The strongest parallel with my work in health care has been in the financial services industry.

There, financial advisors must guide their clients to good decisions about their financial health, just as doctors guide patients to good decisions about their physical health.

Another focus area has been higher education. Educators and student leaders have used my methods to guide young people through many decisions related to their personal and professional lives.

From education to financial services to health care, the common theme is that I have helped professionals guide clients to good decisions.

I have seen the power of critical reflection to improve decisions so that consumers are making informed bets in the face of complexity and uncertainty.

My experiences have led me to develop tools and techniques that professionals can use to reflect critically with clients and thus become more client-centered. I will now share with you what I have learned about:

- five drivers of all decisions;
- three marks of decision quality—to chart your client's course;
- four strategies for critical reflection—and how they can improve client decision quality;
- the FAST process for streamlining critical reflection—so that you can guide clients reliably and efficiently;
- the SLCT process for discovering the client agenda—the opening step in guiding clients to good decisions;
- the SCOPED process for engaging the client in decision support—the closing step in guiding clients to good decisions;
- and a client-centered approach to program design that leverages your extended workforce.

When you integrate these tools and techniques into your practice, you have a new approach to discovery, engagement and leverage. A new DEAL for professionals, including, among others: advisors and architects; doctors and designers; managers and ministers; and teachers and therapists.

The DEAL toolkit is relatively easy to learn and test. To use a cooking metaphor, the first section of this book presents some ingredients of client-centered care. You can eat the ingredients raw. They are delicious and nutritious. The second section presents recipes based on these ingredients. These recipes integrate the ingredients into a richer meal that somehow exceeds the sum of the parts.

Both the ingredients and recipes are based on robust concepts and theories. You can look it up, as they say, in the research literature, where my colleagues and I have published dozens of articles and chapters on the scientific underpinnings of everything contained here. Rigorous studies in medicine indicate that my tools and techniques have been associated with increased patient satisfaction, knowledge, question-asking, and information recall; and reduced anxiety, distress and regret. Researchers have also begun to measure the impact of discovery, engagement, and leverage in areas outside of medicine. Results so far are promising.

My intention is that after completing this book, you'll be able to reflect critically with your clients on what is driving their decisions (Chapter 1). You'll guide them to greater clarity, serenity, and harmony (Chapter 2) through a better balance of thinking, talking, reading, and writing (Chapter 3). You'll accomplish this through a FAST process consisting of divergent (open-ended) and then convergent interactions (Chapter 4) using the SLCT process for discovering and documenting the client agenda (Chapter 5) and the SCOPED process for converging on good decisions (Chapter 6). You'll be able to sustain this in your practice if you implement this program of critical reflection by leveraging all of your resources, including workforce extenders and technology (Chapter 7). I'll conclude in Chapter 8 by reviewing the ways in which we can make a DEAL if you desire assistance beyond the scope of this book.

Let's get started.

Section 1: *DEAL!* Ingredients

The greatest discovery of my generation is that a human being can alter his life by altering his attitudes.
William James

DEAL! Ingredients: Chapter 1

Five Life Drivers

I wanted only to live in accord with the promptings that came from my true self. Why was that so very difficult?
                                                            Herman Hesse

Based on my work with patients facing a health crisis, I have identified five drivers in our lives. These drivers affect client and professional decisions and interactions. Taking stock of these drivers can help you become more client-centered, as you will be able to diagnose what is driving client interests and behaviors, and redirect influences that are driving your clients off course.

The five drivers are: somatic, social, spiritual, soulful, and scientific. I now present them in rough order of influence on our lives.

- Somatic drivers are the body's signals that guide our actions automatically and often unconsciously, including our emotions, reflexes, and instincts.
- Social drivers are the cues we follow from our social environment, in other words people and institutions.
- Spiritual drivers involve guidance from external higher powers.
- Soulful drivers come from our self-image and identity.
- Scientific drivers are the data that we sometimes follow as we consciously weigh the potential consequences of our actions.

Let me illustrate these drivers with a few quick stories about driving, since most of us are familiar with driving automobiles. Later

I'll draw out more explicitly how these drivers relate to professional-client interactions.

Parenthetically, there's a joke about how men are convinced they are experts at three things: driving, decisions, and sex.

That's it. The joke is its own punch line, similar to, "I've got principles, you know, and if you don't like these, I've got others."

Anyway, without awareness of the five drivers, we are just passengers getting whiplash from all the stopping and starting. With awareness, perhaps we can spend more time in the driver's seat engineering our own smooth ride. Gaining some awareness involves a process of critical reflection that I will cover later. First let's review each of the drivers in turn.

Somatic

Experienced automobile drivers are mostly guided by unconscious, automatic processes in their brains and bodies. For example, recently I was driving in rural Northern California and a deer jumped into the road ahead. Without knowing what I was doing, I swerved and avoided a collision. Even though I'm a male driver! That's the somatic driver at work. Instinct. Reflexes. The limbic system. The unconscious mind. The reptilian brain. The lizard brain.

On the flip side, after a few drinks, your somatic drivers can deteriorate to the point that you kill yourself or other people with your driving. Like all the other drivers here, your somatic drivers can keep you on track or throw you off relative to your long-term best interests.

Beyond physical feelings, emotions are also somatic drivers: love, joy, fear, anger, sadness.

With a little practice, you can become more aware of which somatic drivers are operating, and where they are taking you or your clients. For example, Daniel Goleman coined the term "amygdala hijack," referring to the part of our brains that responds emotionally to stimuli, such as when we experience road rage. Just learning that term made me better able to detect and prevent such hijacks. As researchers learn more about somatic drivers, we will better understand their power to amplify or distort our experiences, and perhaps we will be better able to control them.

Social

Social drivers consist of the people, institutions, customs, and other cultural phenomena that influence our decisions as we motor around.

Literally: when I'm backing out of my driveway, my backseat passengers (usually my children) warn me if cars are coming in either direction. That's an example of people driving my decisions. However, social drivers may also be institutional, as when we drive on a pre-arranged side of the road.

Social drivers often operate outside of our conscious awareness, for better or worse. Teenagers may not realize it, but they drive differently when other teenagers are in the car. This has led some states to prohibit teenage learners from driving with other teenagers.

Sometimes the social drivers interact with somatic drivers, such as when some (anti) social person cuts us off, and we respond with road rage.

On a happier note, I drive an unusual car, a bright orange electric Fiat 500. The color matches my hometown San Francisco Giants uniforms. When I see another orange Fiat, I'm socially (and somatically) impelled to smile and wave or give a thumbs up or peace sign, usually in response to a similar friendly hand gesture from the other driver. We pretty much ignore other Fiats. Only the orange electric ones get the salute.

Hand gestures while driving remind me of a time when I was pulling out of a gas station. I had just learned to drive. I was nervous. I paused at the exit. The driver behind me leaned on his horn. I got mad, turned around and gave the "what's up with you?" hand gesture. He honked several more times and gestured back at me.

I couldn't believe what a jerk this guy was. As I pulled out of the gas station, I gave him the "get off my case" hand gesture. He kept honking.

What is this guy's problem? I pulled over to let him pass, and rolled down my window to tell him what time it was. Time to learn some manners! He slowed down and said, "Your gas cap is on your roof." Sometimes we misread social cues and act in ways we later regret.

Happily, user-centered design now means that most gas caps are attached to the car. Did I mention I own an electric car? It doesn't even have a gas cap.

While I'm on this topic of social miscues, I'm reminded of the joke about the English gentleman who boards a train carrying a package of biscuits, his favorite kind, those plain Scottish shortbread cookies. He puts them down on the empty seat next to him along with his newspaper. A Frenchman gets on the train and sits near him, with just that one empty seat between them.

Next thing the Englishman knows, the Frenchman is opening the package of biscuits! He's helping himself! Who does he think he is! Really! The arrogance of the French! The Englishman reaches over, pulls the package of biscuits closer to him, and takes two. That should do it, he thinks. But no, the Frenchman reaches over, takes two biscuits himself, and pulls the package almost entirely over to his side of the empty seat.

Naturally, the Englishman's blood is boiling. But being English, he cannot actively confront such bad manners. Stiff upper lip. He suffers in silence, alternating biscuits with the ill-mannered Frenchman until between them they've eaten the entire package in silence. They travel together a few more hours, and then the Frenchman departs, taking the empty package of biscuits with him. Well, at least he's disposing of his trash, thinks the Englishman. And he reaches over to retrieve his newspaper. Upon picking it up, there he finds his original package of biscuits, waiting to be eaten.

And this reminds me of my all-time favorite joke, because having grown up in Europe, I can attest to its truthiness. Heaven is where the cooks are French, the lovers are Italian, the trains are Swiss, the mechanics are German, and the police are English. In Hell, the cooks are English, the trains are Italian, the mechanics are French, the lovers are Swiss, and the police are German.

Spiritual

Speaking of Heaven and Hell, the next driver is Spiritual. Spiritual drivers show up as we motor along in many ways. My wife keeps a medal of St. Christopher, the patron saint of travelers, in her car because it was her Grandma Benko's, and she believes St. Christopher will keep her safe, or she believes Grandma Benko will keep her safe, or she wants to honor St. Christopher, or Grandma Benko, or both. I'm not totally clear on why it's there. All I know is that there is something spiritual going on. And, anyone who has been to New York City has seen how taxicabs are often shrines to various deities.

Even non-believers have been known to pray to a higher power, or fate, or some other cosmic lottery, for the traffic light to stay green so they will get to their appointment on time.

Ideally we can all express our spiritual beliefs in a motorized vehicle without any downside. However, I occasionally find myself uncomfortable in situations where the driver is ceding all responsibility for the outcome to their favorite deity. Our fate may be in God's hands but please keep *your* hands on the steering wheel!

Spiritual drivers may also operate outside of our consciousness, having become somatically embedded in our habits and practices. Some Catholics may make the sign of the cross reflexively when observing certain events on the road.

I'd like to point out that many of my colleagues in the world of management science overlook the spiritual drivers that may guide a large fraction of the world's population outside of the car as well as inside. I don't think a model of decision making is complete unless it includes spiritual drivers. This has been especially evident to me in working with patients who are facing life-threatening conditions. Dealing with our own mortality generally enriches our sensitivity to spiritual drivers.

Soulful

Soulful drivers stem from our self-image and sense of identity. I have a friend who is from Finland. The Finns are famous for their rally-car champions, meaning drivers who thrash regular cars around mountain routes at high speeds. Therefore, part of my friend's self-image and sense of identity is as a rally-car driver.

I have another friend who prides herself on never having been in an auto collision of any kind. I've been a passenger in cars driven by each of them, and the rally-car ride is quite distinct from the defensive driving ride.

When people navigate decisions driven by their identity and self-image, they are acting formally. Formalism is the philosophical doctrine of taking action based on formal rules rather than consequentialist rules. So formalists don't weigh the consequences of alternative actions. They ask, "What is the rule I must follow?"

I like how one of my Stanford professors, Jim March, articulated it. He said, "Some people ask, 'What will happen in this situation if I do X or Y?'" (That's consequentialism.) "Others ask, 'What kind of person am I, and what does such a person do in this situation?'" (That's formalism.) Our formal commitments to ethical rules often fit into the soulful drivers, although some may come from spiritual sources, and others are more social and a few may be somatic.

Soulful drivers, too, may operate outside of our consciousness. I once read about a depressed woman whose survival drive had fallen very low. She came to realize that she only fastened her seat belt when she felt she was carrying someone important in her car, such as her children. She did not define herself as an important passenger! We may not be fully aware of our self-image even as it drives our decisions.

Scientific

Unlike the other four drivers, we are generally conscious of scientific drivers. That's because I am defining scientific as the process of analyzing data and taking action based on the perceived consequences of different alternatives. Science is indeed the realm of consequentialism.

Learning to drive is a painfully conscious and analytic process. We are told to grip the wheel, lift the right foot off the brake, depress the accelerator, lift the right foot, switch it to the brake. That's a scientific exercise—until driving becomes routine, automated, and ultimately somatic.

Even after driving becomes somatic, automobile drivers may consciously weigh other decisions, such as the risks and benefits of different routes based on the data from the GPS system on our phones or in our cars. We may calculate whether we have enough fuel to get to our destination, or in my case, if my electric car has enough charge. Drivers of electric cars refer to this last phenomenon as range anxiety.

This weighing of pros and cons is a hallmark of consequentialism. In making decisions scientifically, we maximize utility by weighing options and outcomes and choosing the options that offer the best prospect of preferred outcomes. You can see why I have listed the scientific driver last. It has the potential to be incredibly powerful, yet is often last on the list in terms of actual influence on our decisions.

It's not about the car

I've just provided examples from the world of driving automobiles because I'm hoping everyone can relate to them and thereby understand the concepts. However, my canvas is bigger than cars and drivers.

I have several reasons for introducing these five life drivers as the first ingredient in our kitchen of client-centered care. One reason is that professionals tend to dwell in the scientific realm. Your training is highly technical. Those of you who survive the training develop an affinity for all the complexity. Yet most of the time, your clients are operating under the influence of the other drivers. Your scientific guidance may be necessary, but it is not sufficient. You need to acknowledge, embrace, and work in the realm of the other drivers as well.

Acting in your client's interest as well as on their behalf is going to require surfacing, acknowledging, and understanding the full agenda. Not just the scientific issues, but also the somatic, social, spiritual, and soulful dimensions of the client agenda.

For example, professionals dealing with clients may encounter fight, flight or freeze reactions, as when doctors counsel patients who are in shock over a cancer diagnosis. A patient once told me, "Cancer feels like going from immortality to a death sentence." She knew that the diagnosis did not represent such a sharp change in her life expectancy. Yet that is the sense of shock. Professionals can become inured to the crises. They mostly see clients at times of great need, after all. The extraordinary can become routine. Simply acknowledging the client's somatic reactions can go a long way to bridging the distance between professional and client.

Recently a friend brought his parents to see a specialist to advise on how to treat multiple recurrences of a condition called C-diff. The specialist walked in the room, and the first thing she said was, "I've been reviewing your chart. You've been through so much pain and suffering. This must be extremely difficult for you." The entire family was struck by the fact that in all their care to date, this was the first time anyone had acknowledged the somatic pain and distress. My friend emailed me to say, "Today was transformative for my parents. They've never experienced medical care like that ever in their lives." His brother emailed me to add, "I can tell you that Mom and Dad have had incredible peace of mind since yesterday's sessions. My mom, in particular, was struck by just how good caregivers can be."

The specialist did a lot of good things during that visit, but it was the opening acknowledgment of pain and suffering that really touched this family and set a tone of patient-centered care.

Sometimes a client may be having such a severe fight, flight, or freeze reaction that your best response is to defer decisions and actions. This can be counter-intuitive and counter-cultural. For example, in the United Kingdom, the National Health Service has taken initiatives to reduce the wait times for surgery and other treatments. Sounds like a patient-centered initiative, except that in the case of patients facing a cancer diagnosis, professionals are now more incented to move the patient along and book them into treatment as quickly as possible. In many low-risk, early-stage cancers (which includes most breast and prostate cancers, for example), the patient-centered thing to do is to wait for the patient and family to adjust to the diagnosis, and then present options and outcomes, and allow the patient to choose which strategy makes the most sense.

Now, professionals may experience their own somatic reactions, such as a defensive reaction when they feel that their status or knowledge or expertise is being challenged. They may also experience cognitive biases and illusions, such as anchoring on the most recent or most salient case.

For example, I remember one physician telling a patient that she needed to have all her reproductive organs removed in response to a possible ovarian cancer. I suggested the patient get a comprehensive second opinion, which she did. The second opinion recommended monitoring the suspicious lesions on the ovaries for six months before acting more invasively.

The first physician reacted very negatively to this advice, saying, "The last patient I saw like you who did not do the surgery was dead within six months." This patient ended up having the hysterectomy, which showed no cancer. The procedure turned out to have been unnecessary. The physician was in the grips of his own somatic drivers, namely anchoring on a recent case, and reacting defensively rather than scientifically.

To learn more about how somatic and other drivers may distort decision-making, I highly recommend *The Psychology of Judgment and Decision-Making*, by Scott Plous. This entertaining book reviews the many ways that laypeople and professionals alike can be led astray by somatic drivers that evolved to keep us alive in very different environments than the ones we navigate today.

At the same time, highly experienced professionals develop a somatic and unconscious ability to recognize patterns, as described by Gary Klein in his book *Sources of Power*. Another great book on the power of our unconscious is *The Gift of Fear* by Gavin DeBecker. The research on unconscious decision-making was nicely summarized for general audiences by Malcolm Gladwell in his book *Blink!*, while the definitive work in this area, *Thinking, Fast and Slow*, is by a Nobel-prize winning psychologist, Daniel Kahneman. I've listed complete citations for these and other sources that have influenced each chapter of *DEAL!* in a bibliography at the end of this book.

Overall, the limbic system, which is the root of somatic drivers, is both a friend and foe to the experienced professional. The discerning professional will seek to reflect on when to trust somatic drivers and when to challenge them.

In addition to somatic drivers, professionals also need to understand the social drivers influencing their client decisions. I see tremendous influence, for better and for worse, from family members when patients are facing major medical decisions.

Likewise, professionals must reflect critically on their own social drivers: how they are influenced by their peers, and by the financial and other conflicts of interest that arise from social arrangements.

Regarding soulful drivers, professionals need to understand that client self-image matters, and will almost certainly differ from the professional's view of what may be appropriate.

Finally, professionals need to understand how spiritual factors may be driving their own decisions or those of their clients.

Ethical considerations

The five drivers influence every dimension of our lives. This includes ethical dilemmas, where each driver contributes to our assessment of what is morally right or wrong.

Somatically, most human beings have a response of revulsion to certain behaviors that we collectively want to inhibit.

Socially, the cultures we create and live in tend to reflect certain norms about right and wrong.

The spiritual realm is a strong source of ethical guidance for most people. The religious impulse seems to originate in our search for guidance about what is right or wrong.

The soulful domain is where the conscience comes into play. We probably develop a conscience as a function of somatic, social, and spiritual influences. Wherever it comes from, we clearly consult our conscience as a matter of soulful introspection. A conscience is vital to our self-image and identity.

Even scientific analysis has a role to play in ethics. Sometimes right and wrong coincide in bundles that feature trade-offs. A rational, deliberate approach may help us find the best way to proceed when there is no dominant alternative.

Implications for professionals

Going back to the premise of this book, this chapter suggests that you can be a more client-centered professional when you listen for, acknowledge, and connect with people on all five of the drivers.

You can do this by inquiring of your clients at any given time: which drivers are operating here? My guess is that most of the time we and our clients are somatically driven. For many of us, the social drivers may be second most frequent after somatic. These may be trumped from time to time by the spiritual and soulful drivers. The scientific drivers, where so many professionals like to focus, are probably last in frequency. However, what's most important is to understand at a given moment, in a given context, what drivers are in play.

As we'll see in ensuing chapters, being aware of the five drivers, and reflecting critically on them, allows us to move from the back seat to the driver's seat. But the first step in guiding clients to good decisions is taking stock of the rich array of forces that are driving their behaviors overall.

Chapter 1 concept map

Whenever appropriate, I will present a concept map summarizing the key *DEAL!* concepts and their relationships. The first map is simple: it shows the five drivers influencing all decisions and interactions, including the client's interactions with the world at large, and with you, the advisory professional.

Somatic, Social, Spiritual, Soulful, Scientific
↓
Decisions

Exercises for the reader

Here are a few exercises to play with:
1. Think of a decision you made recently in your life. Which drivers came into play? How?
2. How has your self-image changed over the years? What decisions have you made recently that you would have made differently prior to this change?
3. Is there a decision you are making (or made) where you know what to do rationally or scientifically, but you just

don't like it emotionally (or somatically)? Can one of the other drivers serve as a tiebreaker?
4. Do you look, spiritually, to a higher power when making decisions? Which decisions? Can you put your finger on what you find comforting or powerful about prayer?
5. Is there a driver in your life that you feel is distorting your behavior and driving you away from your highest calling? What is it?
6. What are the "shoulds" in your life, as in the voice in your head telling you that you "should" do this or that? Where are those "shoulds" coming from—Somatic? Social? Spiritual? Soulful? Scientific?
7. If you were teaching the five drivers to a new audience, what question or exercise would you design for your students? Prepare to administer this exercise to a member of your family or a close personal friend. Now go do it!
8. Call or email or tweet or text or message someone right now and explain one of the five drivers to them.

DEAL! Ingredients: Chapter 2

Decision Quality

Quality is qualitative. That's why it's called quality. Otherwise, it would be called quantity.

@jeffbelkora

It's important to recognize that most of the time the five drivers lead all of us along a benign life path. However, as a professional, you tend to see clients in crisis. When your clients are confused, anxious, and conflicted about what to do, they likely have come to a crossroads and are getting crossed signals from the five drivers. The somatic, gut reaction may conflict with social advice, while their spiritual or soulful guidance points them in yet another direction, and their scientific mind is overloaded.

When you attempt to guide such clients through their crisis, do you guide them to good decisions or bad? How can you distinguish? Answering this question requires a definition of decision quality.

I propose that we can recognize good decisions from the state of grace we experience when the five drivers align. Somatically, socially, spiritually, soulfully, scientifically—all drivers point in the same direction. This state of grace is marked by clarity, serenity, and harmony. Briefly, clarity is knowing what to do; serenity is the confidence that you've chosen wisely; and harmony is knowing you have the support you need to move forward with your decision. To illustrate these concepts, I will review how one of the patients in my decision support program described the process of arriving at a good decision.

Life and death decisions

I run a patient support program that provides educational materials and services to help physicians guide their patients to good medical decisions. For example, we send patients valid information tailored to their condition so they are not left to their own devices on the internet. We also supply student interns to help patients list questions and make notes and audio-recordings at consultations, because we know that otherwise patients freeze up, forget to ask all of their questions, and forget many of the answers they do receive. This way, our health care professionals address the questions on the patient agenda; and patients can review our notes and recordings as often as needed to absorb complex information.

Here's a patient, Mary, describing the exact moment in which she and her husband experienced clarity, serenity, and harmony. Her story emphasizes how these marks of decision quality can be achieved even in the face of uncertainty that will never go away. My patient support program had provided her with an audio-recording of her discussion with her oncologist. After reviewing the recording, Mary called me. Naturally, I asked permission to record her comments so I could review them. I've transcribed them below and highlighted her unprompted references to clarity, serenity, and harmony; or conversely, confusion, anxiety, and conflict.

> There was a point in the whole conversation where it became **clear** what we wanted to do. And you can hear that on the tape, that's the thing that's so amazing. At that point, my husband and I turned and looked at each other. That was the moment, **both of us knew what we were going to do.** This was a **good decision** for us.
>
> And we were pretty tired, it was about seven in the evening by the time we left the clinic. It had been a long day. But we were able to listen to it

again on the way home. Because by the time we'd actually put the CD in, which was about Burlingame, we'd already had **two arguments** about other points in the discussion.

That was huge, because I don't process things the same way that my husband does. So we went back and listened to that content right then, and it made a huge difference for us, in terms of **not second-guessing** the decisions that we had made.

We had decided not to do chemo, based on the results and based on what Dr. Melisko said. But there's always **that little part in the back of your brain that says, you know, did I do the right thing?** Being able to listen to that part of the conversation again, when we knew that was the right thing to do, really has helped us reinforce that over time. We've listened to it since then.

Mary used the language of decision quality to describe the feelings she experienced with her husband surrounding this decision. I highlighted the key phrases in the passage above and will now note the corresponding elements of decision quality. "It became clear [clarity]... it was a good decision for us [harmony]... we'd already had two arguments [conflict/harmony]... not second-guessing [anxiety/serenity]... little part in the back of your brain that says, did I do the right thing [anxiety/serenity]?"

You can use clarity, serenity, and harmony as a checklist with your clients to test whether your guidance is improving their decision quality. Realistically, your clients are not always going to have the quasi-epiphany that Mary describes having with her oncologist.

Sometimes you have to make a decision and move forward without full clarity, serenity, and harmony.

I've found, though, that clients highly value making incremental progress on these dimensions. Someone stuck in confusion, anxiety, or conflict will be very grateful for partial clarity, serenity, and harmony. Occasionally, you will help your clients experience breakthroughs. But don't let the perfect be the enemy of the good. In bad situations, incremental progress is worth celebrating.

Clarity

Clarity is knowing what to do, given your personal goals and priorities. Achieving clarity is complicated by the uncertainty about the impact of possible actions. First, you don't know what events will occur after you take action. Second, you can't necessarily forecast your own reaction to events if they do occur. Third, you can't be sure that your current goals and priorities will be in place when future events occur.

Nevertheless, when facing all this uncertainty, you can still find clarity of action, either because the five drivers align in one direction serendipitously, or because you reflect sufficiently on your goals and priorities, and gather enough information to make an informed bet on which direction is best to follow. Although you may never resolve the uncertainty, you can transcend your confusion about what to do. I'll have more to say shortly on the process of critical reflection.

Serenity

I define serenity as knowing that you've chosen wisely, meaning you are confident in the process you followed to arrive at your decision, and are confident in the validity of the inputs. As the Serenity Prayer states,

> God, grant me the serenity to accept the things I
> cannot change,

The courage to change the things I can,

And the wisdom to know the difference.

In my more grandiose moments, I see my work on decision making as helping people to answer the Serenity Prayer—along the lines of "God helps those who help themselves."

In the context of decision-making, the Serenity Prayer points out that you can often summon the courage to wrest the steering wheel from the five drivers and consciously improve on their initial, often unconscious, influences.

For example, has your process consisted of pure fight, flight or fight reaction? Have you followed a lazy impulse? These are somatic reactions. But you may be able to summon other somatic reactions, and get your limbic system aroused for vigilance and additional due diligence. Have you gathered additional information (scientific driver), sought the advice of experts (social), and allowed time for introspection (soulful) and prayer (spiritual)?

In terms of gathering information, are you obtaining high quality information? I define good information as inter-subjectively verifiable, meaning that it holds up under cross-examination because enough people have attempted to falsify the information—and failed. By this definition, the scientific method generates good information over time because of its devotion to replication and transparency.

Serenity is the peace of mind that comes with knowing you've expended every effort to make a good decision, and you are ready to place your bet and move forward with no possibility of regret, even if things turn out poorly in ways that are out of your control.

Harmony

Harmony is the support and resources you need to carry out your well-informed, well-considered decisions. I'm in favor of conflict during decision deliberations. Like Abraham Lincoln, we should surround ourselves with critical thinkers and conflict while making decisions. And we may need to revisit decisions critically when we apprehend new information. But at the time we take irrevocable action, for example after deciding to have surgery, we want all parties and resources aligned, and all the wood behind the arrow.

I see productive and unproductive forms of this dynamic play out all the time in health care. Sometimes patients don't experience enough conflict in the decision making stages. They find a doctor whose recommendation sounds right to them, and they go with it. That's OK for little decisions. But no physician makes any major decision without seeking multiple opinions. A study by Newman and colleagues (see bibliography) showed that a multidisciplinary review changed the treatment recommendation in 77 of 149 cases reviewed (52%).

Conversely, once a patient has clarity about what treatment to take, and is making the decision based on valid information and well-considered preferences, I don't like to see family members or health care providers creating conflict. Get behind the decision and make the best of it. The CEO of the startup company that I co-founded used to say it was his job to move the company from one moment of certainty to another.

Harmony is a balancing act, because decisions often can and should be revised as circumstances unfold. You do still need to be adaptive. As John Maynard Keynes said, "When the facts change, I change my mind. What do you do?"

Driving clients to clarity, serenity, and harmony

I want to share with you a brief case study in using the five drivers as a diagnostic and prescriptive tool for guiding clients to clarity, serenity, and harmony. Living as I do in the San Francisco Bay Area, I have a lot of friends who are entrepreneurs. You can't throw a rock here without hitting someone who has started a company. Recently I was speaking with a serial entrepreneur. A serial entrepreneur is someone whose first or second or third company did not become Google or Facebook, and so he or she keeps starting new companies.

Indeed, my friend Jerry started one company and sold it for around $200 million. Even by Silicon Valley's inflated standards, this is a solid hit. But Jerry jumped right back in the saddle to start a new company. This one seems to be going even better than the first, to the point where suitors are knocking, offering to buy the company. Jerry thinks he could sell it now for something in the higher hundreds of millions of dollars. On the other hand, he and his investors believe that if they play their cards right, this company could grow to multi-billion dollar valuations.

In this case, all the possible outcomes are good, but Jerry is still experiencing some confusion, anxiety, and conflict about this dilemma.

He asked me, "Should I sell?" This question could be approached scientifically. That is perhaps where a financial advisor would begin. Instead, I walked him through the five drivers, arriving only last at the scientific driver.

Somatic—what is your gut feeling? Do you have the stomach to continue? Do you feel a thrill about continuing the fight, solving the puzzle, pursuing the quest? Or do you dread it? Jerry's answer was unequivocal: bring it on. He is hungry for the challenges ahead.

Social—who wants him to sell? Who wants him to hold? What signals is he getting from all the social drivers? Jerry thinks this one is mixed. One employee keeps dropping not-so-subtle hints along the lines of, "Jerry, if you were to sell this company for a lot of money, my family would be very grateful." Jerry thinks this is a fine reason to sell a company—a windfall can represent financial security, college educations, housing, and other benefits for early or senior employees. On the other hand, Jerry has assembled a great team that is working well together and up for more challenges ahead.

Spiritual—what does God want Jerry to do? What is God's plan for Jerry? Jerry doesn't think God really factors into this decision.

Soulful—what is Jerry's self-image? Is he a serial entrepreneur who builds companies up to a few hundred million and then sells them? Or is he someone who wants to build a large, enduring company that lasts generations and moves entire fields or markets? Jerry's self-image favors "go big or go home."

Scientific—what is the business case for selling versus holding? In financial engineering terms, what is Jerry's estimate of the probabilistically weighted, discounted, net present value of future cash flows associated with selling versus holding? Jerry thinks the expected (probability-weighted) value of selling is higher. However, the distribution of financial values associated with holding has a long tail to the right. He has a company in a great market that is growing; his team is terrific; the technology is working well. Having made a fortune already, Jerry may now be more risk-seeking than risk-neutral or risk-averse, in the sense that he values the lottery ticket associated with rare but very positive outcomes at higher than its expected value.

Overall Jerry found that reflecting on the five drivers clarified his decision. The market opportunity, combined with his soulful aspiration to build a large, enduring company, and his somatic appetite for the fight ahead, drove him to press on. His sense of confusion, anxiety, and conflict dissipated—and he enjoyed a state of greater clarity, serenity, and harmony.

The five drivers go to college

Recently I was teaching a group of college students about the five drivers. I asked for an audience volunteer, and a young woman stood up and described a personal dilemma she was facing. I talked her through applying the five drivers and thought I would share this transcript with you as another example of how you might verbally walk someone through the use of this framework.

> Dora: Hey guys, my name's Dora, like the Explorer. I actually am really confused on my decision because it feels like each option has something that the other one doesn't. This is an internship decision for the summer. And one of

them is working at Walter Reed because I'm from the area, and that's in my profession, and it's close to home and it's paid. And then, the other one is working for a pharmaceutical company out in China. I've always really wanted to travel. I've been to Southeast Asia before and I love it there. It's not paid though, and I have to pay for my flight, and the expense of living there. And then, we have a family friend who asked if I wanted to intern for him in the international division at the CIA. And that has absolutely nothing to do with what I want to do, but I mean—who passes that up? So I just have no idea.

JB: You know when you said that you had different options, I was kind of skeptical. I was thinking, they're probably not that different. These are very different. Well it turns out there are five drivers of all of our decisions. If we pay attention to what these five drivers are, we might be able to harness them and put ourselves in the driver's seat, okay? I'm just going to go through them first—five of them. So the first one is somatic. The somatic driver—soma means the body. Some people refer to making decisions based on their gut or their instinct. Generally, that's like the limbic system, your nervous system, some people call it the reptilian brain. It's the oldest part of our brain. And it's very good at unconscious decision making. When you sleep on a decision, that's what's happening is your somatic forces are working on it, and your brain unconsciously is going through all kinds of pattern recognition to figure out, is this something that makes sense for me? So that's often a very good use of your time and resources, to actually sleep on it and come back to the decision.

The second driver is social, and this refers to all the advice you might be able to get, or the information you might be able to get from peers—these things can be by the way either positive or negative. Sometimes social drivers are pushing you in a way that's actually not really in your interest but that is in other people's interest.

The third driver is spiritual, which is when you're making a hard decision, a lot of people turn to a higher power, and pray or appeal in other ways, or even use intermediaries like clergy or other representatives of their faith or religion, wiser voices, experienced voices. So that's another way to break the ties and start to get to the clarity that I was talking about.

The fourth category is soulful. As opposed to spiritual, which is looking outside at a higher power, soulful is looking inside at your identity and your self-image and what kind of person are you, and what does that kind of person do in such a situation as this? So it's really coming at the decision from a slightly different perspective.

And then the last one is scientific, and the scientific is a little bit more of, let's weigh the data. Let's look at the facts, let's look at the figures and let's be really rational about it. And actually a lot of decision scientists in my field focus on this. But I put that last because in a lot of ways, often you're going to get to decisions through the others.

So let's run through these with you. ==Somatically, sometimes you can hold up your feelings, your emotions, your sense of what might make you happy, and just project that forward on these decisions.== Is China going to make you happy? How are you going to feel there? Walter Reed—is that going to make you happy being there? Is working in the CIA, is that going to be some kind of crazy adventure that makes you happy? Is there any feeling you have about those three so far?

Dora: I mean, I love to travel, so the whole China thing really interests me. As far as the other two, I mean, Walter Reed is obviously an awesome experience. There's all parts of them that make me so intrigued, and I'm just—I want to do that!

JB: Yeah, okay, so this first category is the physical feeling that you get when you contemplate it, and just talking to you, it sounds like China wins on this category.

Dora: Yeah.

JB: Maybe not on the others, but that the thrill of adventure and travel is what appeals to you. And everyone else in this room is going to be totally different on how they respond to this kind of an opportunity. It's important not to let other people's signals conflict with yours. You've really got to pay attention to your body and your signals on things like this. So if we drop down to the Social, are there social reasons to prefer one over the other? Is the person who's introducing you at the CIA, could they be a long-term mentor? Or at Walter Reed or any of these other places, is there anything like that? Or do your parents really want you to do something and you want to honor that? Sometimes you don't, sometimes you need to push back. Sometimes you want to. Do you have any feeling?

Dora: Definitely staying local would help with the connections and everything, because I do know somebody with one of the internships, and through that you meet so many other people. And it's like six degrees of separation and who knows who I'll meet, which is definitely one of the reasons I want to stay local. So I think in that sense I would be more inclined to either lean toward one of the other, probably look at the CIA because you can do just about anything, they don't care what your major is. You know, if they want you, they want you.

JB: Let me ask you a personal question—are there any significant others in the picture that you need to—

Dora: You mean, like boys? No, I'm single.

[Laughter]

JB: Okay.

Dora: Sorry if that was a little rude, and flippant!

JB: That's something to pay attention to at your age and stage in life, whether you're a boy or a girl. Well, later in life, is that going to be different?

Dora: Yeah.

JB: And so, you can start thinking about a decision like this as, is there one of these options that I might not be as able to take advantage of later in life? So, does that—

Dora: Absolutely! That's why I want to do China because I mean, I'm not tied down to anything. I mean my parents will miss me, I guess, but they'll be there forever.

JB: Okay, I'm going to put China in the second category. So far, China's doing pretty well underneath the first two drivers. Then there's the Spiritual dimension. And sometimes decisions like this may not be particularly spiritual. But if, if there is a component of that, or if you find prayer, or advice from people in your faith important, is there anything like that in this case?

Dora: I definitely do, yeah, and again the China comes back just because there's something that draws you to being able to push yourself to a limit. I won't know anybody there, you know, that's going to be a completely new place I've never been before. It's definitely going to challenge me.

JB: And I think your parents are going to be praying for your safety—when you're that far away, right?

Dora (laughter): They'll be fine.

JB: Okay so, on the soulful dimension, this is a pretty interesting one for, I think, all of us to consider, which is your self-image. Now, you guys are in a period in your lives—this continues probably longer than you might expect—of identity formation. So, maybe you don't have a fully formed self-image, but maybe there's an aspirational self-image, or maybe you already have a self-image. Are you the intrepid traveler? Do you have a self-image around being a spy and a secret agent? Do you have a self-image around, Walter Reed sounds altruistic and helping people. There's no value judgment here. You have to make the value judgment. Other people may have value judgments on it but this is for you to make a value judgment on. Do you have a sense of one of those?

Dora: Yeah. In that case it would definitely be Walter Reed just because China is working with a massive pharmaceutical company so it's not very personal. It's a massive manufacturer kind of thing, whereas Walter Reed, I mean you work with other agencies in my area and you get to be a lot more hands on with people.

JB: So on the soulful sort of identity, self-image level, it's that altruism and public service that's calling to you there. And then on the

Scientific approach, if you sort of weighed data, and facts, and figures and think very cold-bloodedly and analytically and rationally, is there one of them that would be the best career move for you?

Dora: Career move would probably be China too just because it implements that whole travel, sense of adventure that I want but it also is the industry that I would probably want to get into. I have a business minor and it's a very business-oriented trip, it's just going to cost a lot.

JB: And that may be where the scientific angle also comes in, is you want to get out a spreadsheet and really figure out the cost perspective, and really get a good budget going. The scientific mind would also start to think, can you fundraise for it, or get gifts from parents or relatives, or you know, whatever, what can you do to support that? So, China looks pretty good on a lot of these. I would also say and as a mentor or a coach to anyone, that it's admirable to want to be altruistic. However, you can sometimes also invest in yourself and be altruistic at another time in your life. As I said, sometimes the flexibility to do something like go to China might be at its highest now as opposed to later. I don't have a view, I'm just trying to reflect back some of the insights from going through this. So does this help?

Dora: Yeah, I mean, it's clear what I'm leaning toward now.

JB: And sometimes you just need to give yourself permission to go for it. You know, the word decide comes from two roots in Latin and Greek, and they mean similar things: to cut away and to kill. I think about this as being a warrior about your decisions, you're cutting away and you're killing alternative futures. That sounds negative, but really what you're doing when you're saying no to things and you're cutting them away, is you're increasing your yes to what you do choose. So, a lot of times there's a fear of missing out about all the other things I'm saying no to, and I encourage you to think like warriors about this, and when you make a decision, kill the other options and really go for the one you're going after, and just increase its value by being fully engaged and fully committed to it. And thank you so much for sharing that.

In reviewing this encounter, please note that Dora went from being "really confused" about her decision to "clear what I'm leaning toward now." Again, guiding clients to good decisions is a matter of helping them navigate away from confusion, anxiety, and conflict and toward clarity, serenity, and harmony.

Ethical considerations

My work promotes the view that professionals should seek to advance the client agenda and help people achieve clarity, serenity, and harmony. In endorsing this view, I assume that your clients are law-abiding, responsible, and pro-social. Outside of law enforcement professionals, most of us don't often encounter many people who willfully and wantonly want to break the law, act irresponsibly, or transgress against moral standards.

Sometimes, however, you will encounter clients who are about to stray from a legal, ethical, and prudent path. You may be able to use the tools in this book to help such clients reconnect with their longer-term agenda. For most people, taking a long view will forestall any temporary and misguided deviations from the straight and narrow.

In rare cases, you may reach a limit in which being client-centered is the wrong thing to do, because your client's agenda remains malicious, illegal, or immoral. In that rare occurrence, your fiduciary responsibility includes an escape hatch for exceptions. You will need to escalate the issue and ask other parties to help you handle the exception.

This will be challenging, but you can turn some of the tools I am teaching you back on to yourself, and pursue your own clarity, serenity, and harmony in resolving the matter.

For example, one of the most conflicted times in my life was when I uncovered what I felt were unethical actions by colleagues at work. I lost sleep for many nights pondering what to do. I started to feel more serene after consulting a human resources expert who pointed me to a reasonable process. I read about the applicable laws and found the exact codes that had been violated, gaining clarity. Then I consulted colleagues who pledged their support. Suddenly I was sleeping fine: clear, serene, and in harmony. I was able to confront my colleagues and ultimately reverse the harm. It was still challenging, but far less so than if I had reacted impulsively myself. I knew that I needed to get to clarity, serenity, and harmony; and this knowledge spurred me on to productive action.

Implications for professionals

I started this book by quoting George Bernard Shaw to the effect that you are at risk for conspiring, however inadvertently, against the laity. In Chapter 1, I suggested that one specific risk factor could be your tendency to approach clients with a professional, scientific mindset. Your clients may be under the influence of other decision drivers, such as somatic, social, spiritual, and soulful forces.

As you diagnose the interplay of forces, I've proposed in Chapter 2 that you can assess whether the client is closer to clarity, serenity, and harmony—or confusion, anxiety, and conflict. In other words, what is the quality of their decision making, under the existing balance of the five drivers?

While acknowledging and honoring all five of the drivers, your next move will be to engage your clients in critical reflection to improve the quality of their decisions. That is the topic of the next chapter. We will see that you can help your clients think, talk, read, and write in a more balanced and productive way. This will tend to increase their clarity, serenity, and harmony.

Chapter 2 concept map

The key concepts in Chapter 2 are clarity, serenity, and harmony, which I propose as the state of grace to which we all should aspire. The five drivers from Chapter 1 often lead to clarity, serenity, and harmony, but professionals are likely to encounter clients facing confusion, anxiety and conflict. Sometimes such clients can improve their condition by themselves. At other times, they need you to help them harness the five drivers in a quest for clarity, serenity, and harmony. The concept map below shows how the five drivers may lead clients to a positive or negative decision-making experience.

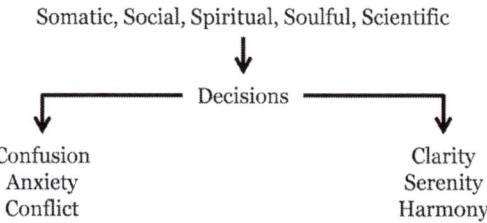

Exercises for the reader

1. Think of a time when you felt turmoil in your life about what to do next. Was it because you were unclear? Or because you lacked serenity about the process you were following? Or was it that the people you relied on for next steps were in conflict about whether they would support you?
2. How about a time when you went to an expert for advice and came away feeling clear, serene, and supported? What did the expert say or do that improved your decision quality?
3. Now how about a time when you went to an expert and came away feeling confused, anxious and conflicted. What did that expert say or do that reduced your decision quality?
4. Flip these exercises from the client to the professional perspective. When you encounter clients who are stuck, how many of them are stuck primarily because the complexity of the situation is confusing them? How many are stuck because they are not following a process that gives them serenity? How many are stuck because they don't have the support they need to act in accord with their preferred path?
5. Next time you are speaking with a client, explain clarity, serenity, and harmony. Ask them to rate, on a scale of 0 to 100, their current level in each of these dimensions. Then focus your coaching on the area where they are most stuck.

DEAL! Ingredients: Chapter 3

Critical Reflection

I write so I can see what I think.

Mark Twain

All five drivers can be positive or negative influences in our lives at various times and in various situations, leading us toward or away from clarity, serenity, and harmony. I find the scientific driver very compelling because, used judiciously, it can liberate us from whiplash in the hands of the other four drivers.

In this case, I'm not referring to science in terms of blindly following quantitative data. I'm referring to critical reflection and analysis, which of course may be qualitative as well as quantitative.

Specifically, as an ethical professional, you can increase your client-centeredness by helping your clients reflect critically on their decisions; and by reflecting critically on your own behavior.

What is critical reflection? I've identified a particularly simple way of operationalizing this abstract concept. The way I define it, critical reflection involves thinking, talking, reading, and writing as a means of generating new insights on which to act.

Can we agree that when I say thinking, I mean consciously thinking, what Kahneman calls slow thinking, as opposed to unconscious or automatic thought? More poetically than Kahneman, the BrainWise curriculum refers to this as Wizard Brain versus Lizard Brain.

Talking means conversing, which includes listening.

Reading includes reviewing all sorts of audio-visual material. You could call it researching, but that's less poetic.

And I'd like to stipulate that writing will include other forms of symbolic manipulation, such as sketching or coding.

Thus we can refer to these four strategies in extremely familiar shorthand, like the three Rs's of reading, writing, and 'rithmetic. Thinking, talking, reading and writing.

As with the five drivers, I like to keep my frameworks pretty simple and pragmatic. In any given situation, you can diagnose how much your clients are thinking, talking, reading, and writing. I recommend making sure they have achieved a good balance.

Recently my former student Margot wanted to move to Oakland in order to be closer to her medical school rotation in the East part of the San Francisco Bay Area. She identified several housing options with various tradeoffs in terms of room-mates, cost, convenience, safety, and so forth. She struggled with the decision of which housing option to choose. One night as she lay awake, she recalled my strategies, and slapped her head: "Margot! I've been thinking about this decision, and talking about it, and reading about it but I haven't been writing about it!" So she got out of bed and wrote about it and immediately figured out what to do.

Like Margot, many of us toss and turn at night thinking about a problem, and may even talk it over with someone. Talking it over often helps, but we may get to a point where we are talking in circles, or getting conflicting information or advice from our interlocutors. At that point, we should check whether the sticking point or conflict is something that can be empirically resolved through research—missing but knowable information. Usually, research will help you converge on new insights. You can accelerate the convergence by writing or journaling your thoughts, discussions, and reading. As Mark Twain supposedly said, "I write so I can see what I think."

I will now present each of these strategies for critical reflection in more detail.

Think

Recall that the drivers often operate through our unconscious. This means we may navigate our journeys without much awareness of which way the wind and tides are driving us.

This may not matter in most situations. Decision scientists have contrasted satisficing to optimizing. We satisfice when we simply (and lazily) verify on some level (perhaps somatically) that the path ahead satisfies some minimum desired criteria, in which case we take it as good enough. We optimize, consciously, when we work hard to assure that the path ahead is the best possible path.

But since the drivers operate on an unconscious level so much of the time, we are at risk of under-thinking in high stakes situations such as major purchases or big decisions about our health and wellbeing. We may not recognize the high stakes and we may remain in our barely conscious, satisficing state. We go with the flow.

For example, I have a friend who had gall bladder surgery because a surgeon told her that was what she needed. She proceeded with the operation, and reflected critically on her decision only after experiencing complications and side effects from the surgery. She was used to trusting experts who presented reasonable sounding solutions to diagnosed problems. Part of my professional mission in life is to activate patients to reflect critically on all medical decisions, before agreeing to any treatment.

At other times, we recognize that the stakes are indeed high enough to warrant critical reflection, but it's as if our minds have a defense mechanism against getting too close or spending too much time on that topic precisely because we are vulnerable. Paradoxically, that is exactly when we may benefit the most from hard thought.

I feel that in my life I've benefited from hard thought about where to go to graduate school; switching degree programs; getting married; whether to undergo vision correction surgery; finding a job; buying a car; buying a house; choosing a mortgage; refinancing our mortgage; having children; and making decisions about the health and well-being of my children. Most of the time, I did not want to buckle down and think hard about these issues. However, I believe some hard thinking made a big difference, as I reflected on who I was, where I wanted to go in my life, and how best to get there.

Admittedly, once you start thinking, you begin to run another risk: overthinking. I define overthinking as driving scientifically (using consequentialism) when we should be relying more on the other drivers.

For example, take dating. When I was younger I had a terrible time breaking up with girlfriends. I would overthink it in a big way. Then I learned a three-step breakup method from my friend Joe. I can't remember the first two steps, and neither does he anymore, but it doesn't matter because the third step is the only important one. You just tell the person, "It doesn't feel right." Then they say, "What doesn't feel right?" You say, "I don't know. Going out with you just doesn't feel right." "What am I supposed to do with that?" "I don't know. It just doesn't feel right. I need to break up with you because going out with you just doesn't feel right." There is no arguing with "it doesn't feel right"! It's a somatic driver.

One of my former students just gave me a book about decision making of a different sort. It's called *The Life-Changing Magic of Tidying Up*. The author, Marie Kondo, describes a foolproof mechanism for getting rid of stuff. Typically we overthink a decision about whether to discard an item, even one we don't use much or at all. Instead, she recommends you touch each item and test, while holding it, whether it evokes the somatic emotion of joy. If it does, keep it. If it doesn't, discard it. Thank it for teaching you about your tastes and preferences, and let it go find someone who will appreciate it more.

Another example of overthinking: we may be in organizations where we have taken on a fiduciary responsibility to serve the organizational agenda, or client interests, or the public. This is true for doctors, for a category of financial advisors known as fiduciaries, or for officers in a fraternity, sorority, bank, law firm, the Army, Navy, Air Force, Marines. Well, suppose one of our colleagues has violated the oath of office in some way. In most cases, there's a clear policy for handling violations. That's a formal rule that should be driven by self-image, not consequentialism.

Indeed, if we start thinking consequentially, thoughts come in to our heads like, "This is my friend, blowing the whistle is going to have negative career implications." That smacks of overthinking. In such cases, the right thing may be to simply apply the policy. I'm especially sanguine about doing this when all parties joined the organization voluntarily. If you are an officer of a fraternity or sorority and your friend hazes someone, and hazing is disallowed by your charter, what is there to think about? Blow the whistle, apply the sanctions, and get on with life. No need for a lot of anguish when you are applying formalist rules.

So critical reflection involves thinking like Goldilocks: not too hot, not too cold, but just the right amount.

Talk

We have all experienced the benefits of talking through our concerns about a crossroads. Often speaking to someone else, or even thinking out loud, generates new insights.

As an example, consider this story about my friend and former colleague, Robert. Robert once ran the engineering department of a Silicon Valley technology firm. He knew that programmers often get stuck while working on code, which affects quality and productivity. If the programmers interrupt other programmers to ask for help, that may resolve their issue but interrupt the productivity and quality performance of the other programmers. So Robert installed a stuffed monkey in a side alcove of the office and made the following rule. If you get stuck, before you email or talk to anyone else, you have to go explain your problem, out loud, to the monkey. "Go tell it to the monkey," he would say. Most of the time, that was sufficient. People thinking out loud often arrive at new insights.

Incidentally, I used to find it frustrating when certain friends or family members or colleagues would interrupt my own flow to think out loud. This was especially frustrating to me when the person doing it was a person in a position of authority. I felt obliged to hear them out. I learned to be patient with them, and myself, simply by reminding myself, "They are thinking out loud and that is helping them sort their thoughts out."

As a result of Robert's insights, I give myself permission to think out loud to myself if no stuffed monkey is around. I now routinely do this in the car and in my office. Sometimes I record myself thinking out loud, not so much because I want to review what I have said, but because it makes me feel more like I am thinking out loud to another person.

When I really want another person to hear my think-aloud sessions, I make a conscious effort to seek permission. I'll say something like, "I would like to think out loud about something with you. Is now a good time or should I check back later?" At least that way, I'm less likely to interrupt their flow.

Read

Reading about a decision or problem is easier today than it ever has been, thanks to the internet. However, through inertia or laziness or a sense of being overwhelmed, we often fail to take advantage of the internet or other resources for doing research. Or we give up after an initial search generates too much information for us to make sense of quickly.

My experience has been that high stakes situations deserve a lot more research and due diligence than we usually give them. Decision scientists have a rule of thumb that you should spend one to ten percent of the value of a decision on actually analyzing the decision. So, for example, if you are contemplating buying a car, and figuring on spending somewhere between $20,000 and $30,000, you should spend somewhere between $200 and $3,000 actually analyzing that decision.

Now, some of that expense might be the value of your time spent online or traveling to show rooms and taking test drives. You should think of that time as a significant portion of your budget for doing research. You might also buy specialized subscriptions (like Consumer Reports) if needed; or hire an expert intermediary, such as Cartelligent.

Now imagine that the stakes are higher, such as you are deciding whether or not to have elective surgery, such as knee replacement. In a rough and ready sense, the value of that decision is at least the time you might spend recovering and rehabilitating; plus all of your out of pocket costs.

Sometimes people protest that there are high stakes emergencies where there just isn't time to do research or read about the situation. In practice, I think this is quite rare. When my daughter was born, her medical team wanted to perform a spinal tap to test for meningitis. This was a frightening prospect for my wife and me. While we were waiting for a specialist to arrive, I pulled up an internet search and within five minutes had developed a list of informed questions. There is a longer story here, the short version is that my daughter was fine and a little research went a long way. Some emergency rooms have signs that state, "This is a matter of life or death. Time is of the essence. Everybody slow down."

In safety conscious domains, such as aviation, people make extensive use of checklists. Consider the famous Miracle on the Hudson. A crew landed an airline safely on the Hudson River after a collision with birds that rendered both engines inoperable. You can access the transcripts of the cockpit recordings from this incident online, as a matter of public record. We all can learn a lot from reviewing this kind of incident. Here I would like to hone in on some of the excerpts that include references to reading. For example, before and during the emergency, they were reading checklists, which represent codified lessons learned from prior incidents. I've bolded those interactions in the excerpt below:

> PA-2 ladies and gentlemen at this time we're number one for takeoff, flight attendants please be seated.
>
> 15:19:25
>
> HOT-1 * *.
>
> 15:19:27
>
> **HOT-2 takeoff min fuel quantity verify. nineteen thousand pounds required we got twenty one point eight on board.**
>
> 15:19:32
>
> HOT-1 nineteen thousand pounds required, twenty one eight on board.
>
> 15:19:35
>
> HOT-2 flight attendants notified, engine mode is normal, **the taxi checklist is complete sir.**
>
> 15:26:52
>
> **HOT-2 flaps up please, after takeoff checklist.**
>
> 15:26:54
>
> HOT-1 flaps up.
>
> 15:27:07
>
> **HOT-1 after takeoff checklist complete.**
>
> 15:27:10.4
>
> HOT-1 birds.
>
> 15:27:11

HOT-2 whoa.

15:27:11.4

CAM [sound of thump/thud(s) followed by shuddering sound]

15:27:12

HOT-2 oh

15:27:13

HOT-1 oh yeah.

15:27:13

CAM [sound similar to decrease in engine noise/frequency begins]

15:27:14

HOT-2 uh oh.

15:27:15

HOT-1 we got one rol—both of 'em rolling back.

15:27:18

CAM [rumbling sound begins and continues until approximately

15:28:08

HOT-1 my aircraft.

15:27:24

HOT-2 your aircraft.

15:27:24.4

FWC [sound of single chime]

15:27:25

CAM [sound similar to electrical noise from engine igniters begins]

15:27:26.5

FWC priority left. [auto callout from the FWC. this occurs when the sidestick priority button is activated on the Captain's sidestick]

15:27:26.5

FWC [sound of single chime]

15:27:28

CAM [sound similar to electrical noise from engine igniters ends]

15:27:28

HOT-1 get the QRH... [Quick Reference Handbook]

loss of thrust on both engines.

Here are two aviators, in the middle of a catastrophic loss of power, with just minutes until they crash-land, and the senior of the two tells the junior to consult the quick reference handbook on the topic of loss of thrust in both engines. This is after they've made extensive use of written checklists.

Why? Because reference guides codify lessons learned; and in an emergency, memories lapse; and there are no second chances. Again, that is why the signs say: "This is a matter of life and death. Time is of the essence. Everybody slow down."

When I speak to professionals and others with important responsibilities, I often ask whether they download key documents and checklists to their phones for easy access. For example, on college campuses, fraternity and sorority leaders are held accountable to certain policies and procedures promoted by the insurance industry. Insurers have published a reference guide with checklists for dealing with many critical incidents that do occur in fraternity and sorority life, such as when visitors are injured in a residential facility. If I were a fraternity or sorority president, I would have that reference guide downloaded to my phone, and at the first sign of trouble, I would skim it over.

There's an expression in Silicon Valley: RTFM, for Read The Freaking Manual. As the aviation industry illustrates, even in time-critical emergencies, the best use of your time may be to consult a checklist or manual. Why? Because such reference guides often contain the distilled wisdom of past failures and near-failures, as well as successes. Culturally, we tend to associate stopping to read something as a sign of delay, whereas in fact it may be a sign of astounding acceleration toward a more robust solution.

Write

I write so I can see what I think. I cite this aphorism repeatedly because audiences resonate so much with it, and it becomes a useful reminder when things get tough.

Writing allows us to externalize our thoughts. When we have externalized our thoughts in symbolic code, we can manipulate that symbolic code. We can change the sequence, priority, and logic of our thoughts. We can rearrange them spatially and elaborate on them.

All this puts us in the driver seat relative to our thoughts. Again, I include sketching and other forms of coding (e.g. spreadsheets and computer programs) when I use the term write.

Another reason to write, sketch, and code is that we relieve the burden on our short-term memories, which are famously limited to retaining seven plus or minus two items.

When I was a graduate student, I experienced a vivid demonstration of the power of writing. A professor at Stanford, Ron Howard, posed a challenge to the entire auditorium of 200 students, as he often did, Socrates-style.

This one was something along the lines of, "If you know the probability distribution of A and you know the distribution of B, can you say anything about the chance that A is greater than B?" Professor Howard structured our responses debate style, asking people to speak to the yes and then the no view. Then he took a vote to see what the class believed.

Seeing that the class was divided after the first vote, Professor Howard asked students to stand and elaborate on what their peers had said to persuade the opposition. He continued doing this until virtually the whole class had concluded one way, and was arguing against a solitary holdout, who argued the other way.

Professor Howard concluded the exercise by pointing out that the solitary holdout was correct, and that no one had thought to come to the chalkboard (yes, chalkboard) and draw a decision tree or other picture. When our professor sketched a basic logic diagram, the answer was immediately obvious. (Can you figure it out?) Both of these lessons stuck with me for life. The minority may be correct; and you should always use all of your resources, including sketching or writing.

To this day, I'm amazed at how people neglect this aspect of critical reflection. Since experiencing Professor Howard's demonstration, I keep a whiteboard in my office, and hold meetings in areas where there are whiteboards. Many offices today have walls that are themselves whiteboard surfaces.

Yet some of my favorite leaders have no whiteboard or similar surface in their offices. They have meeting areas—chairs, a table. Just no whiteboard. So I carry a notebook and pen wherever I go.

I also carry electronic mobile devices with powerful word processing software, but I've noticed that none of them are very good for creating disposable sketches. I've been convinced of the power of disposable sketches since reading Malcolm Gladwell's essay in the New Yorker entitled *The Social Life of Paper,* which recounts how air traffic controllers use disposable sketches to improve their work.

Not writing, coding, sketching, or marking can have severe consequences. Recently I arranged to observe a complex surgery involving several surgeons from distinct subspecialties. Before the surgery, I asked one of the surgeons whether he used checklists or huddles or time outs or whiteboards or any of the other methods currently under adoption by quality-focused physicians. Many of these methods have been in broad use in another high-stakes sector, the aviation industry.

My colleague said, "Oh yes, we used to do all that stuff where I trained. But now, you know, I can keep track of it all in my head." About two hours later, this surgeon caught the other surgeon's eye, pointed to a detached part of the patient's body, and said, "Where did that come from?" Each of the surgeons denied having removed this quivering mass of flesh. Neither knew where it came from or where it belonged. Luckily the patient survived with no harm done.

One of my engineering friends left Stanford after a master's degree in systems engineering, and went to medical school, eventually specializing in neurosurgery. Early in his residency, he was rounding with a senior physician who was pointing out complex features of some case. My friend took notes in a notebook he carries with him everywhere to facilitate critical reflection. He noticed he was the only one taking notes. Then the physician called him out. "Ian! What are you doing?" "I'm taking notes sir." "Why?" "So I can review them later." "I'll [expletive] tell you when I want you to take [expletive notes.] Put that [expletive] away and just [expletive] listen to me!"

The Institute of Medicine estimated that avoidable medical errors kill 44,000 to 98,000 people each year in the United States, which equates to one commercial airline crash killing all passengers every day of the year. In comparison, the Aviation Safety Network reports that the commercial aviation industry killed 265 people worldwide in 2013. My examples suggest that a culture of thinking, talking, reading, and writing contributes to a strong safety record in aviation. Conversely, a lack of critical reflection in medicine contributes to fatal errors.

Checks and balances

Thinking, talking, reading, and writing are powerful strategies for critical reflection, even taken alone. There is even more power in paying attention to the balance among them. People often do one or two of these but rarely employ all of these critical reflection senses. When you are stuck, try one of the modes you've been neglecting.

Personal finance example

My own personal examples of high-stakes decisions include: going to college and graduate school; getting married; having children; buying a house; refinancing the mortgage on our house; making personal and family health decisions; planning for retirement; and making career changes.

In all these decisions, having markers of decision quality have helped me play the long game. I've avoided some of the negative consequences of acting impulsively or prematurely in matters that affect my relationships, finances, appearance, or other potential trapdoors in our complex web of life.

I have learned not to prematurely override confusion, anxiety, and conflict. These are signals from the five drivers that all is not well. We ignore them at our peril.

Finally, a balanced approach to thinking, talking, reading, and writing has been transformative.

To give one specific example, when I joined UCSF, my wife and I stretched to buy a house in San Francisco. We were pretty strapped for cash, so we explored entering into a variable-rate mortgage with the first three years fixed at an exceptionally low rate. This rate would vary starting in year four based on a reference interest rate linked to bond prices and currency exchange rates in a complex formula. Our mortgage broker told us the name of this index that would determine our monthly payments after the three years of teaser rates. The broker described this as a great way to reduce our monthly payments and free up cash that we sorely needed for other expenses.

The variable mortgage was, however, complex. We were definitely confused by it, as well as anxious and conflicted. So we talked about it some more with our broker, and thought about it. That really didn't help much. And then I had the good sense to go read about the specific index.

I found a website devoted to tracking and analyzing this index. It turned out that a large part of the formula was a moving average of previous months. A practical ramification was that we could get a preview of where our payments would be heading in the fourth year, by watching this index and forecasting the range of possible future values it would take based on the prior years.

That would give us a preview of the possible jump in payments upon exiting the low fixed-rate period. That opened up the possibility of exiting the mortgage after three years and avoiding the variable rates. However, we were told that it would cost us $15,000 in prepayment penalties to get out of this mortgage.

This was the source of additional confusion, anxiety, and conflict, because we had to weigh the possibility of a big jump in the variable rate interest, four years out, against the value of fixed low rates, factoring in a $15,000 prepayment penalty.

Overall, we were concerned about the risks involved with the variable rate mortgage, yet that mortgage, along with some down payment assistance from our parents, was what could make our house affordable for our budget. We did not want to pass on this house and get priced out of the real estate market for many years, which can easily happen in a heated market like San Francisco.

We were tempted to move forward and ignore the confusion, anxiety, and conflict, because the whole situation was so complex. But we did not want to wing it on such a high stakes decision. We held out for more clarity of action, more serenity about the process we were following, and more harmony.

We had thought, talked, and read about the mortgage. Now it was time to write. At times like this in my life, I've been especially grateful for my quantitative training in systems engineering. I coded a spreadsheet. I ran the numbers. I ran multiple scenarios and simulated them over 5, 10, 15, and 30 years, factoring in the possibility of paying a $15,000 prepayment penalty if the variable rate suddenly skyrocketed.

My wife and I both ultimately felt pretty serene about my calculations and projections. We were clear that this was our best path to owning a home, while keeping expenses down for a few years while we built our careers. After some reflection, we had each other's support for this calculated risk.

With such major decisions, you can't expect total clarity, serenity, and harmony—either for yourselves or your clients. In this example, my wife and I did experience some ongoing anxiety. That's a good somatic signal that you need to remain vigilant. During the initial three year fixed rate period, I carefully read the underlying interest rate that would prevail starting in year four, and updated my projections regularly.

It turned out that we signed our mortgage at the lowest rate in the 50 year history of this particular interest rate index. It started to rise much faster than we had projected. Some of our confusion, anxiety, and conflict returned. There was no way we wanted to pay the $15,000 prepayment penalty! Yet a high variable interest rate could send our monthly payments through the roof starting in year four of our mortgage.

Again we were patient and disciplined in our quest for clarity, serenity, and harmony. Unfortunately, the first experts we spoke with tended to lead with a strong bias one way or another. Either these variable rate mortgages were the work of the devil and we should get out as quickly as possible; or we would be crazy to pay such a large prepayment penalty.

With a little more reading and research, we learned a few things that helped us return to clarity, serenity, and harmony. We found that the prepayment penalty could be rolled into our next mortgage. Since we planned to live in our house a long time, and we felt San Francisco real estate was a good bet, we felt OK about increasing our loan amount and spreading the prepayment penalty over 30 years.

In addition, we learned that much of the prepayment penalty could be written off as interest payments on the mortgage. This turned the $15,000 sum into a much more palatable amount, which we were then able to finance over 30 years. We locked in a fixed 30 year mortgage at a very reasonable rate.

We've since refinanced that again to drive our monthly payments even lower. In doing so, we placed a relatively clear, serene, and harmonious bet on the long-term prospects for San Francisco real estate. We freed up some cash for the other things that are so expensive in San Francisco. We could still lose this bet. But we arrived at it in a high quality way. And we used all of our critical reflection faculties in a balanced way—thinking, talking, reading, and writing.

I'm aware that this example is a little confounded by the fact that variable rate mortgages played a huge role in financial collapse in the United States, as banks made irresponsible loans and consumers made irresponsible decisions. This topic actually stirs up strong emotions, as it may be doing for you while you read this.

I am also aware that I am a quant geek and not everyone has the ability or desire to build spreadsheets for personal decisions. My larger point is that when you're dealing with complexity, thinking and talking are not sufficient. You must also read and, crucially, write, to achieve clarity, serenity, and harmony.

Pet decisions

I want to offer a lighter example, one that does not have the historical baggage of variable rate mortgages, or spreadsheets, which may have clouded your view of the underlying lesson in decision quality. This is another illustration of arriving at a good decision through a balanced approach to critical reflection.

As we built our family, like many, we faced decisions about acquiring pets. This was the source of much drama, or in my terms, confusion, anxiety, and conflict.

I was the source of most of the conflict. I am deeply committed to my wife and children, as well as to my professional mission at work. I did not want to take on any more responsibility. I knew that the projections of certain family members about the impact of pets on my life were founded on optimism rather than experience, and that any relatively high-maintenance pet would require my attention. I was reluctant to make that commitment at that point in my life.

I could have tried to unilaterally shut down all discussions about pets. Or, my wife could have come home one day, as some spouses do, with a puppy or kitten or other relatively high-maintenance pet. Either way would probably have meant more conflict over time.

In this as in all matters, I knew there was clarity, serenity, and harmony somewhere out there if we pursued it patiently enough. So we thought and talked, but also did some reading and writing.

I wrote out my criteria for what constituted, in my view, a truly low-maintenance pet. For example, I wanted a pet that could live in the backyard, and that we could leave unattended on weekend trips.

My children checked out various animal books from the library and researched whether each proposed pet would meet my criteria.

Long story short, we ended up raising backyard chicks. They are low-maintenance enough to meet my criteria for not requiring too much of my attention, because we can leave them in their palatial backyard coop unattended for days at a time if necessary. At the same time, they meet our family desire for pets. And we get delicious eggs.

And we were able to roll the monthly payments on their coop into our mortgage and deduct the interest! Just kidding, Mr. Taxman.

Other family examples

Writing is particularly underused as a mode of critical reflection. The other day, my son was stuck on a math problem. I told him to recopy the problem word for word. He resisted: "How is that going to help? Anyway, I can do this in my head." I insisted that he write it out. As he was copying the problem over, he said, "Oh, now I get it." I pointed out that my advice had worked. He said, "No, the answer just came to me." I said, "Any time you are stuck, try just writing the problem out and see if the answer just comes to you."

Likewise, when my daughter is stuck on how to spell a word, I ask her to picture reading the word in a sentence in a book and then try writing it. One day, she was stuck on how to spell "deceitful." I knew she had read all the Baby-Sitter's Club books. So I said, "Picture in your mind the sentence: 'The baby-sitters were deceitful.'" She said, "That word never happened in the Babysitter's Club." And then she spelled it perfectly.

Chapter 3 concept map

To recap, we've seen how five drivers may lead clients to or away from clarity, serenity, and harmony in their decision-making. The last of these drivers, the scientific driver, is special because we can use it to reflect critically on our decisions. There are only four strategies or behaviors involved in critical reflection: thinking, talking, reading, and writing. Generally we practice only one or two, to our detriment. We can improve the quality of critical reflection, and of our decisions, by engaging in all four strategies in a more balanced way. The concept map below shows when and how you, the professional, may want to intervene with your clients. When they come to you in a state of confusion, anxiety, and conflict, work with them on a balanced strategy of thinking, talking, reading, and writing.

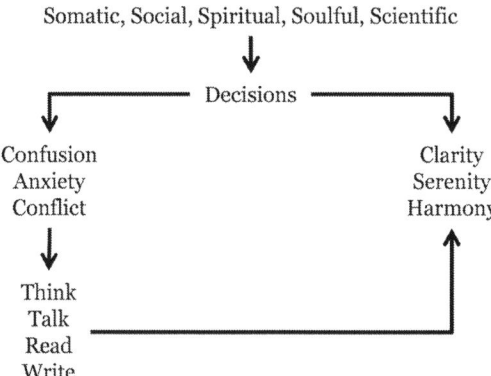

Exercises for the reader

Review the inventory that follows, and select a decision you made recently that was significant to your life. Of the time you spent analyzing this decision, what proportion did you invest in thinking? In talking? In reading? In writing? Next time you make a decision, try investing the same amount of time in each modality of critical reflection. Check in with your clients as well. You'll find most are doing some thinking and talking, but not much reading and writing. You can help them rectify that.

Belkora Decision Inventory

1. Career path (college major, internships, gap year, grad school, profession, professional development)
2. Civic engagement (run for office, vote, contribute, volunteer, serve)
3. Education (apply to college, grad school, select school, loans, study abroad, stop, drop, transfer out)
4. Entertainment (mobile, voice, data, TV, cable, internet)
5. Environment (consumption, recycling)
6. Family planning (abstinence, contraception, children)
7. Finances (saving, spending, investments, insurance)

8. Health and wellness (diet, exercise, prevention, wellbeing)
9. Health care treatment (accidents, disease)
10. Housing (rent, buy, share, where)
11. Marriage (vows, agreements, monogamy, fidelity, divorce)
12. Parenting (decisions for and with your children)
13. Personal technology (computer, tablet, smartphone)
14. Recreation (creative, artistic, hobbies, sports, travel)
15. Religion, spirituality
16. Social life (friends, dating, use of social networking)
17. Transportation: Buying, leasing, renting, sharing wheels

DEAL! Ingredients: Chapter 4

FAST Critical Reflection

Get clear on what you are talking about before you say anything about it.

Ronald A. Howard

In the course of my research, I have found that simply attending to the balance between thinking, talking, reading, and writing goes a long way to improving the quality of decisions. Using all of these scientific modalities to reflect on the other drivers (somatic, social, spiritual, soulful) usually results in progress toward clarity, serenity, and harmony. This is the core concept in *DEAL!*

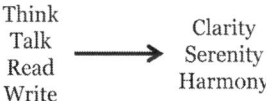

Likewise, you should find that when you guide your clients through these four strategies, they tend to report greater clarity, serenity, and harmony. It's a big payoff for a small investment.

With a slightly larger investment in structure, I have found that I can accelerate and amplify progress toward high quality decisions. I will describe a structured approach to thinking, talking, reading and writing in this chapter.

My prescription for additional structure originates in the observation that, regardless of how many inputs there may be to a decision, it results in only a small number of actions. In health care, patients can change their behavior, take medicine, have surgery, or rely on a new device. Sometimes the treatment is a combination of the above. Still, that is a small number of actions that emerge from something as complicated and emotionally trying as, say, a diagnosis of cancer.

The implication is that decision-making is a convergent process. We must converge on action from a broad funnel of inputs, namely the five drivers: somatic, social, spiritual, soulful, and scientific.

Yet if we converge too quickly, we often miss out on clarity, serenity, and harmony because we have not assimilated and accommodated all the inputs from the five drivers.

My experience suggests that we cannot converge immediately as we think, talk, read, and write. Rather, we can converge only after a period of exploratory or divergent thinking, talking, reading, and writing.

Over the years, I've crystallized this insight into a process inspired by other problem solving techniques which advocate *divergence* before *convergence*. Mine is called FAST. It's a way of sequencing your thinking, talking, reading, and writing with a client, as illustrated in this concept map fragment:

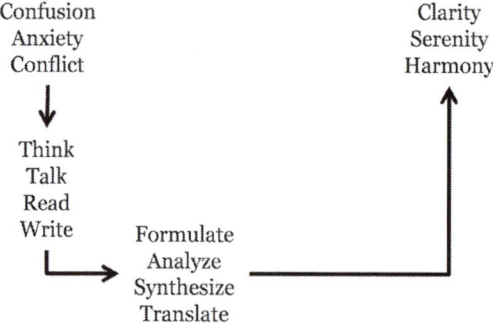

FAST stands for formulate issues, analyze issues, synthesize insights, and translate insights into action. These FAST steps are roughly sequential, with opportunities to loop back. They correspond to divergent thinking in the formulate phase, followed by divergent and convergent thinking in the analyze step, and finally more convergent thinking in the synthesize and translate steps. Here's a flowchart showing the sequence of steps in FAST, and their associated work products:

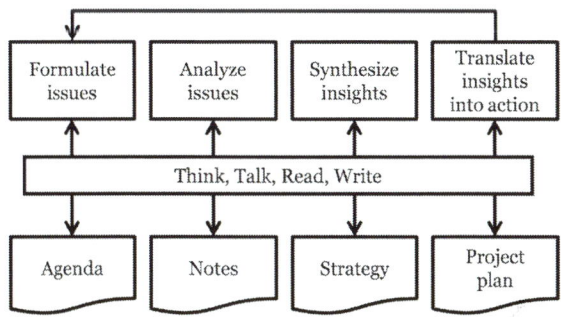

Because we must balance thinking, talking, reading, and writing, each of the steps in the process generates a written work product. In the formulate phase, we generate an agenda or list of issues, concerns, goals, priorities, and questions. This agenda establishes the object or target of further thinking, talking, reading, and writing.

In the analyze phase, we are operating on our issue list, transforming and rearranging and elaborating on the issues—as well as perhaps generating new issues through a process of association. In this phase, we produce notes documenting our analysis. These notes serve to make our thinking, talking, reading, and writing more transparent, so we can hold each other accountable for critique and improvement.

In the synthesize phase, we are looking to make progress, gain insights, and perhaps even achieve a breakthrough. We generate a summary of our thinking, talking, reading, and writing. I sometimes use storytell as the S in FAST instead of synthesize because synthesizing insights generally means telling ourselves a new causal story that we believe is more robust and productive than the last.

Finally, we must translate insight into action. Quite often the action may be to reformulate the problem, because we arrived at an insight that reframed our initial issue list. Then certainly we must iterate. Eventually, though, we are ready to articulate and execute concrete plans for action. At this stage, we produce some kind of project plan to serve as a roadmap and to help diverse parties coordinate.

FAST thus gives us a sequence to follow as we think, talk, read, and write to reflect critically on our decisions.

In my experience, it's important to keep the four strategies in balance at every step of the FAST process. I will now elaborate on each step.

Formulate issues

Early in the process of critical reflection, it's important to allow for divergent thinking, talking, reading, and writing. Most problem-solving techniques involve a period of brainstorming. In the formulate step, we give ourselves permission to formulate and generate issues. I like the word "issue" because it is neutral. It connotes some topic that we feel is relevant to the situation at hand. During this formulation phase, we may also want to surface concerns, priorities, goals, questions. They can all be labeled issues. While in generation mode, they need not be terribly concrete or specific. They can represent placeholders or bookmarks for later elaboration. Later I will refer to this formulation phase as the discovery process—as in discovering the patient or client agenda.

Analyze issues

In the middle stages of critical reflection, we can drill into the issues we've formulated. This can be divergent or convergent. For example, we may elaborate on the early issues in ways that generate more issues, which is divergent. Or we may elaborate on them to make them more concrete, which can be convergent. We may cluster or group related topics (convergent), put them into a sequence (such as chronologically or by priority, also convergent), or array them in a mind map or flow chart or directed graph (convergent) to indicate relationships between issues.

Synthesize insights

Synthesis or storytelling or summarizing is the art of generating and explaining insight. I am using the word insight to mean deep understanding about the issues you previously formulated and analyzed.

With deep understanding, you understand the dynamics of the issues at hand. In other words, you understand not only the current, static state of the issues, but also how a change in one issue may change your view of another issue. With insight, you begin to understand what are the key issues driving the overall system of issues.

In that sense, deep understanding means you can focus your thinking, talking, reading, and writing on a smaller set of critical issues, while appreciating the interdependence of these issues with the overall system.

If I may lapse into mathematical jargon for a moment: insight is knowing the partial derivatives of the system output with respect to each individual input. Having even just a first-order understanding of dynamics in a system represents tremendous insight. On the rare occasions we may get to an appreciation of the second or third order dynamics, we have achieved very deep understanding of the system.

Conventionally, there is no magic bullet for synthesizing insight. After immersing yourself in formulating and analyzing issues, you are supposed to wait for insight to emerge—the blinding flash of understanding. This is most welcome when it occurs. And indeed sleeping on things will often promote a eureka moment, thanks to the somatic driver.

However, I have often found it possible to make progress simply by *reaching for insight:* by attempting to distill the system of issues into something simpler and more essential.

I first came to understanding the importance of reaching for insight from my quantitative training in systems engineering. There I learned that many systems follow the Pareto principle, in the sense that eighty percent of the variation in a system usually comes from twenty percent of the variables. If you can identify those 20% of the variables that are driving most of the variation, you can understand most of the system dynamics. In quantitative analysis, we do this by building quantitative models that simulate the system, and then conducting sensitivity analysis to identify the key variables.

In qualitative analysis, reaching for insight can be nothing more complicated than attempting a summary. We can summarize via three of the four strategies: thinking, talking, and writing. Don't forget that writing includes drawing pictures, sketches, flowcharts and the like as well as coding spreadsheets or other computer programs.

In addition to synthesizing insight from summarizing the issues overall, you may wish to reflect on the five drivers mentioned earlier. Sleeping on an issue list, you may find your limbic system guides you to insight somatically. Socializing the issue list, others may point you to insight. Praying to a higher power, or meditating, may lead you there spiritually. Introspection about your self-image or your aspirational identity may help. All these can be in aid of the scientific driver, represented by your earlier attempts at conscious issue formulation and analysis.

Sometimes when deep insight is elusive, we must proceed incrementally and reach for progress rather than leap to insight. I track where I am in generating insight by asking myself: am I regressing and things are getting more complicated, not simpler? Am I stuck on a plateau? Am I making progress? Have I generated new insight? Have I achieved a breakthrough? If I've regressed, this usually means I need to go back to more formulation and analysis.

I'm reminded of the adage:

> We have not succeeded in answering all your questions. The answers we have found only serve to raise a whole new set of questions. In some ways we feel we are as confused as ever, but we believe we are confused on a higher level, and about more important things.

I'm also reminded of T.S. Eliot's lines: We shall not cease from exploration/And the end of all our exploring/Will be to arrive where we started/And know the Place for the first time.

Indeed, sometimes a breakthrough will lead to reframing the entire situation, and thus going back to the formulation stage to identify new issues and then analyze them.

Once we have synthesized or summarized our insights, we may need to further refine how we explain them to others. We should avoid the trap of thinking that to explain, we must take our audience back through all the formulation and analysis steps.

To illustrate this point, my Stanford professor Ron Howard used the act of breaking into a house as a metaphor for solving a problem. When you break into a house, you find a weak point such as the coal chute. Located around the back, the double doors open down into the basement. This is where people once delivered and deposited coal for the furnace.

You might break in through the coal chute and emerge dusty and dirty into the basement. But when you are bringing other people into the house, do you make them go through the coal chute? No, you go to the front door, unlock it from the inside, polish up the door handle, and invite in your guests.

In other words, analysts must tell a coherent story using the insight, rather than explain to people how analysis generated the insight. Telling people all about the origins of a solution can amount to dragging them through the coal chute. Bring the audience through the front door.

The work product for the synthesis phase is therefore a story summarizing your insights and their implications.

Translate insights into action

Gaining insight tells us what road to ride. Yet we will not get to our destination on insight alone. We must still drive down the road. Thus we must translate our insights into action. The product of this phase is some kind of plan.

Once again, we should use all four critical reflections strategies to develop the plan: thinking, talking, reading, and writing. Writing occupies a special place in this pantheon because we can so easily share our thinking through symbolic code, which allows anyone to critique and refine our plans.

Therefore one product of the translation phase is a written plan, and the actions that flow from it. Ideally we will continuously fine-tune and improve our plan. I favor an approach called discovery-driven planning, which suggests that we set a direction (based on insight) and then continually update our plan based on what we discover as we move forward. This approach has caught on recently with agile software production methods and adaptive design philosophies.

The way I implement discovery-driven planning is to write out the steps for implementing the decision, and an initial schedule, along with an issue list. Similar to agile approaches in product development, I make sure I am marching in the direction of my goals, while dealing with issues along the way. This requires frequent communication among the members of a team tasked with implementing a decision.

FAST forward

I'm committed to practicing what I preach. Some years ago, I began assiduously following the FAST process when making my own consumer decisions for medium to large ticket items. I've seen good results, but more importantly, my wife has noticed an improvement. I used to be a sucker for any Swiss army knife solution to a problem. In other words, I would try to find a single product that had a lot of functionality, but often didn't do anything very well. This is how we ended up, in the late 1990s, with a portable television slash cd player slash radio boom box.

After inventing FAST, I followed the process with my decisions and ended up with better solutions to various challenges. For example, I've developed the family-friendly but extremely time-consuming habit of making photo books as gifts for each of my children on their birthdays. This requires sifting through thousands of photos taken over the past year; selecting a hundred or so; and laying them out in photo book software. The payoff is that the entire family enjoys browsing through the photo history of our children's lives, collected in a couple dozen nicely bound volumes.

Reviewing the photo books never fails to trigger laughs and happy memories. I realize we could accomplish something similar in a digital format, but the photo books are tangible, colorful, and easy to access and browse from the shelves next to our fireplace in the living room.

Because the production of each photo book takes a month of my evenings and weekends each year, I'm pretty motivated to invest in making the process as efficient and effective as possible. So, when it came time to purchase a new digital camera recently, I followed my own advice. Instead of my usual approach to technology purchases—endless amounts of online browsing in the hopes of eventually converging on a dominant alternative—I paid attention to balancing the four strategies of critical reflection in each of the FAST stages.

In the formulation stage, I wrote out the scenarios or use cases for the camera. I am serious enough about this hobby that I don't consider smartphones to be viable contenders, mostly because of ergonomics—I can't hold my phone and snap photos comfortably and effectively, compared to a camera.

Taking extra time in formulation, and being patient with the divergent thinking in that stage, led to some surprising revelations. It turns out, on reflection, over the years, that the best photo book entries are impromptu shots of unscheduled events taking place at home. On browsing (reading) through past photo books, I realized that I have taken, in the past, an awful lot of indoor low-light shots at home that turned out relatively poorly—yet featured great content, when we could make out what was portrayed.

In reaching for insight, in the synthesis or storytelling phase, I talked with my wife about the fact that I spend a lot of time transferring photos to my laptop and organizing them on its hard drive. This led me to realize how important the laptop is to my production of the annual birthday books. I translated this insight into a reformulation of the issues. In my reformulation, I conceived of the camera and laptop as interacting components of a birthday-book production system.

This led to additional insights, and ultimately a written list of criteria as follows:

1. Good sensor for better low-light photos.
2. Stores photos on fast, large-capacity SD card—for easiest transfer to my laptop, which has a fast SD card reader built in. I like not having to fish around for a connecting cable, nor do I need to bring one on the road.
3. Camera has rechargeable batteries that charge while in the camera. Recharging the batteries in the camera means that I can leave the camera on the writing table in the living room, connected to a USB charger, where it is always at hand and ready to shoot.
4. Pocketable—the best camera is the one you have with you.
5. Fast start-up time—need to get the first shot off quickly.
6. Shoots video in mp4 format for easy laptop playback and editing.
7. Optical viewfinder if possible in addition to screen.

Reformulating my criteria in terms of a birthday book production system made the final analysis stage quick and easy. In 2014, there were only a very small number of large sensor cameras that stored photos on SD cards, and could recharge using a USB cable—and only one with an optical viewfinder: the Sony RX-100 mark 3.

When translating my insights into action, I got on Amazon and found a great deal on a used RX-100, which a professional photographer had bought for his wife, who didn't use it.

Incidentally, I now purchase protection plans for all consumer devices, not because they are good value economically (they aren't) but because they make more sense to me environmentally. When I have a protection plan, I get the covered device repaired if it breaks, and I'm confident that my broken one will be refurbished and put back into use. When I don't own a protection plan, it ends up being vastly cheaper to replace the broken device than to repair it, and I'm not convinced that my efforts to recycle broken electronics really translate into re-use.

I know some of you are reading this and thinking, "Big deal, he did some research and found the right camera." You're right, on one level no big deal there. What is a big deal is that this specific process of critical reflection is replicable and scalable to higher-stakes decisions, as we'll see in the second section of this book.

FAST-backwards

Above I've used a personal and, I hope, relatable family example to illustrate the power of following the divergent/convergent sequence in FAST. In particular, investments in the formulation phase often pay huge dividends downstream—especially formulating goals, priorities, and criteria.

Unfortunately, my experience with professionals is that you often skimp on the formulating issues phase. This makes some sense. You have a lot of specialized training and you naturally prefer to direct the conversation to your areas of comfort and expertise. Divergent thinking could take extra time and lead you away from your professional agenda.

Conversely, most professionals are happy enough to analyze issues within their domains of technical expertise. Sometimes they fall down again on at the synthesis phase. It takes additional effort to summarize the key dynamics in a client's dilemma, and then synthesize insights. Also, generating insights is risky, because it can lead clients to reformulate their situation, and then you have to go back to divergent thinking!

So I have found that professionals are at risk of neglecting the formulate and synthesize steps, while more comfortable with the analyze and translate into action phases of FAST.

In fact, in my experience, many professionals act FAST-backwards. They start with their recommendations (translating insight to action), then summarize their insights, and finally offer some analysis. They pretty much leave out formulation altogether.

Here's a caricature of a FAST-backwards financial advisor meeting with a client:

> Hello Mr. X, it's good to see you again. I've been reviewing your portfolio, which has been hammered along with the rest of the markets during the recent sell-off. Now, it's very important not to over-react. I'm recommending our usual re-balancing, but generally we want to stay the course with our long term strategy. You don't want to be selling low and buying high. So the only adjustment is I'd like to overweight the international sector a little more over the next year by purchasing more of X mutual funds. Make sense?"

In essence, the professional-centered encounter works backwards through the FAST sequence. The professional opens with a bid to translate his or her insights into a recommended action (e.g. "stay the course"). The professional shares his or her synthesis or summary of the main insights driving the recommendation ("don't overreact... don't sell low and buy high"). And then the professional asks for confirmation: "make sense?"

Who would ever want to start with formulating and then addressing the actual client agenda? Well, someone committed to client-centered care.

Paradoxically, the FAST-backwards model that predominates among professionals likely has backfired on them more than it's worth, and likely will even more in the future as clients demand more client-centered care from professionals.

Decades of research in motivational interviewing show that attempting to control the agenda is a surefire way to alienate clients and in fact push them in the opposite direction. There's a Newton's Law of human interaction that states that every force of persuasion applied in one direction stimulates an equal and opposite response. So when professionals are directive and persuasive, they may win the battle but lose the war. The client may say nothing at the moment, and switch later to another advisor, apparently for no reason.

So why do professionals persist in FAST-backwards? My take is that professionals want to maintain control of the agenda because they really feel they have the client's best interests at heart and need to protect the client from overthinking or rethinking problems that professionals have already solved.

Because rising generations are more consumeristic about their interactions with professionals, FAST-backwards will increasingly result in clients saying, "You're not listening to me." And they will disintermediate the professional—manage their own affairs—or find professionals who do listen.

Now the professional who applies FAST has to let go of control. In my financial example above, the client may choose to sell stocks in a down market, in violation of a previously articulated long-term portfolio strategy. The professional must anchor not on the action taken, but on whether it was fully informed and based on well-considered preferences and a deliberate process. Recall that a good decision results in clarity, serenity, and harmony.

In my example above, the financial advisor could have said,

> Good to see you again. What's on your agenda for today's meeting? Aha, you want to talk about your son's upcoming wedding; your daughter's graduation from college; and the turmoil in the markets. Shall we discuss them in that order? OK, please tell me more about your son's upcoming wedding.

Notice that FAST is iterative as the conversation branches. You must formulate, analyze, synthesize, and triage each topic separately. Having surfaced an agenda item such as an upcoming wedding, you cannot then launch into your views on budgeting the wedding based on a recent experience with a wedding in another client's family. Rather, you must remain in formulation mode, eliciting the client concerns. Perhaps this client has in mind an estate plan triggered by the realization that the son is about to start a family. Let the client tell you!

Many professionals will dismiss my concerns about FAST-backwards as applying to others. "I listen to my clients!" Maybe you do, maybe you don't. Are you really in a position to judge?

My concern in this regard is that professionals, by dint of specialization, have lost the ability to diagnose their own blind spots in communicating with clients. As I will propose in the next chapter, the only way in which anyone can really be confident that they understand their own communication patterns is to record their conversations, transcribe them, and analyze the transcripts. Only in slow motion, and with relatively objective methods, can professionals begin to recognize where they may stray from client-centered practice.

Just to make sure I am offending a wide range of professionals, my caricature or parody of a surgeon meeting a patient reflects similar dynamics.

> Hi Mrs. X, I've been reviewing your chart, and based on what I see there, I'm going to recommend surgery. I have an operating room slot available next week, and I think we should book that because we really don't want this condition to get worse, do we? Now, the reason I am recommending this surgery is that it is very well tolerated, no major risks or side effects, and it should prevent any further spread or recurrence of the problem. Make sense?

My caricature surgeon is also working FAST-backwards: translating his or her insights into action; then summarizing the reasoning; and finally asking for confirmation, which appeals to something called the social agreement tendency we all have to not rock the boat.

Because of a long tradition of paternalism and patient acquiescence, surgeons can get away with FAST-backwards more than other professionals can. Yet even health care consumers are voting with their feet, away from such directive professionals.

What if I told you that there was a way to start with the formulate phase and truly discover and analyze the client agenda? And that embedded in a well-designed program, this protocol would not have to prolong consultations, or cost more resources overall?

Discovering and engaging the client agenda, while leveraging your workforce and technology resources, will be the topic of the next three chapters.

Chapter 4 concept map

The concept map for Chapter 4 shows how the FAST process is simply a way of implementing the think/talk/read/write model of critical reflection. The idea remains to reflect critically on the five drivers, and to make progress toward clarity, serenity, and harmony.

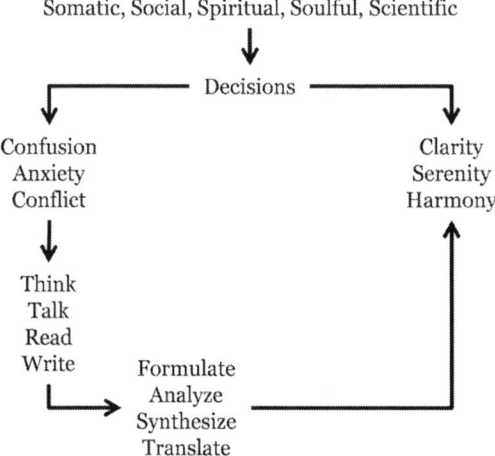

Exercises for the reader

1. Pay attention to how people present their views on what you should do about a dilemma or decision. Do they start with formulating and brainstorming issues? Or with recommendations on how to translate their insights into action? What proportion of time do they spend in each of the phases of critical reflection (formulate, analyze, synthesize, translate)?
2. Now flip the perspective from client to professional. When meeting with clients, do you start with formulating the issues? How much time do you spend in each phase of critical reflection? In what order do you proceed?

Section 2: *DEAL!* Recipes

There is nothing so practical as a good theory.
Kurt Lewin

DEAL! Recipes: Chapter 5

Discovery

Interruption occurred, on average, 18 seconds after the patient began to speak...
> Beckman and Frankel, The Effect of Physician Behavior... Ann. Intern. Med. 1984;101:692-696.

The FAST process is a way of structuring your thinking, talking, reading, and writing as you formulate and analyze issues; synthesize insights; and translate insights into action. I am now going to describe a specific application of the formulation step of the FAST process. I'm referring to discovering the client agenda.

In most advisory situations, the client brings an agenda of issues surrounding a problem or opportunity or decision. What I have learned is that the issues may be unconscious or implicit, as well as explicit. In this way, a client's issues are like an iceberg. Some issues are above the waterline. Clients are aware of them, and are willing to share some of them. But each issue may extend deeper into the water than is initially apparent. And, the iceberg of issues may be broader (wider) below the waterline than above.

On a technical note, the Iceberg Framework extends a model developed by Chris Argyris called the Left-Hand Column. This represented what a client was thinking but not saying during an interaction. Argyris and colleagues also invented a technique called the Ladder of Inference, which asks clients to elaborate on their verbal statements in the hope that they will disclose more of what is in their left-hand column.

In my model, the left-hand column is the part of the iceberg below the waterline. The client may not even be consciously aware of the depth and breadth of the iceberg. Happily, the way consciousness works, clients can retrieve or construct most of the iceberg through critical reflection, in other words through thinking, talking, reading, and writing. I have developed the SLCT (pronounced "select") process for surfacing the whole iceberg.

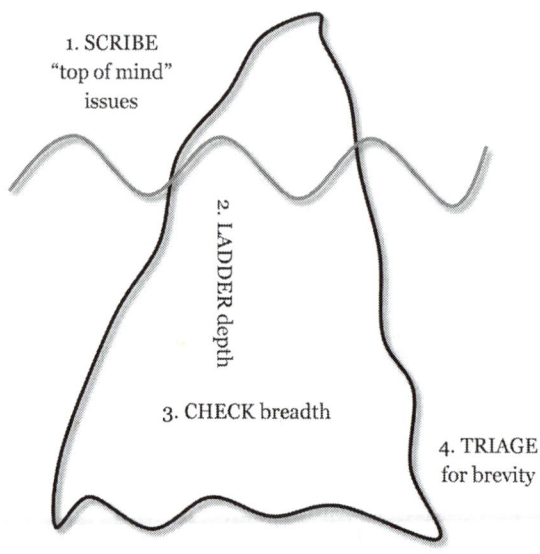

SLCT

SLCT stands for scribing, laddering, checking, and triaging. Please consult the iceberg graphic above for a schematic of how these strategies can be used to probe the iceberg, representing the client agenda. Triaging includes categorizing. I discuss categorizing as if it were a separate step in what follows, but for the purposes of the SLCT acronym it belongs with triaging.

In the first step, scribing, the interviewer simply prompts the client to list all the issues of relevance to some specific problem or opportunity. The idea is to get what is at the top of the client's mind, or at the tip of the iceberg. The interviewer writes or scribes without interrupting until they've generated an initial issue list. Due to the limits of working memory, clients generally will articulate seven plus or minus two issues. In the second step, laddering, the interviewer asks the client to elaborate on any of the scribed issues that lack specificity. In the third step, checking, the interviewer stimulates broad new responses from the client by administering a checklist of prompts. Finally, the interviewer creates a word-processed version of the client agenda, triaging for clarity and brevity.

I will briefly illustrate the overall process with the example of a patient, recently diagnosed with breast cancer, who listed her initial questions and concerns with a student intern in my patient support program:

Version 1—Scribed
1. Do I need chemotherapy?
2. I want to continue working if I need chemotherapy.
3. How much will chemotherapy help me?

In the second step, laddering, the interviewer asked the client to elaborate on each issue in the initial list. The interviewer went back into scribing mode, listening without interrupting and writing additional issues down under each item in the initial list. The elaborations represented going deeper into the iceberg, surfacing issues below the waterline. This produced version 2, an elaborated version of the initial scribed list.

Version 2—Laddered
1. Do I need chemotherapy?
   a. If I need chemotherapy, what are the options?
   b. What does Dr. Oncologist recommend and why?
2. I want to continue working if I need chemotherapy.
   a. Work occupies my mind.
   b. I work with kids, I am concerned about my immune system getting weakened by chemotherapy.
3. How much will chemotherapy help me?
   a. I would like to understand the benefits vs. risks of chemotherapy.

b. I would also like to learn about recovery and side effects of chemotherapy.

In the third step, checking, the interviewer used a checklist or set of prompts to stimulate broader client disclosure of issues. The formula is for the interviewer to say, "You've told me about X, Y, and Z. I've listed those. Sometimes people in your situation also have other concerns. For example, what about A? What about B? What about C?" Now the interviewer scribes the new issues separate from the laddered list, creating a checked list.

Checklists will generally vary according to the professional domain. One checklist that works across multiple domains is past, present, and future. Using this checklist, the interviewer simply asks if there are any other issues on the client's mind (or agenda) related to the past (e.g. medical history), present (e.g. treatment options) or future (e.g. treatment outcomes).

In my breast cancer example, the patient responded that she did have more to say about each of these topics, and the interviewer duly scribed her comments as follows:

Version 3—Checked
PAST
- I was diagnosed with breast cancer in August and had surgery a month later, followed by radiation.

PRESENT
- I want to understand the following terms on the pathology report:
  o Moderately differentiated infiltrating carcinoma?
  o Surgical margins free of tumor—does that mean that there is none for 1/2 cm around edges?

FUTURE
- If I end up doing a brutal kind of chemotherapy, I want to get it on a Friday to recover so I can go back to work on Monday.

- Can I get treatment somewhere closer to home? Are there any local oncologists Dr. Oncologist would recommend?
- I have a friend who will drive me up here on Fridays if necessary. My daughter is supportive.

Finally, in the fourth step, triaging, the interviewer merges all the issues in versions 2 (laddered) and 3 (checked) into version 4 (triaged), categorizes them, and edits for brevity and clarity. This produces a one-page, word-processed document of bullet points divided into subheadings. Here is the scribed, laddered, checked, and triaged document from my patient example. The interviewer used the topic headings from the checking stage to categorize all of the items from the laddered stage as well. Below, I've indicated in square parentheses the origin of each agenda item.

Version 4—Triaged

PAST
- I was diagnosed with breast cancer in August and had surgery a month later, followed by radiation. [V3—Checked]

PRESENT
- I want to understand the following terms on the pathology report: [V3—Checked]
    o Moderately differentiated infiltrating carcinoma? [V3—Checked]
    o Surgical margins free of tumor—does that mean that there is none for 1/2 cm around edges? [V3—Checked]
- Do I need chemotherapy? [V1—Scribed]
    o If I need chemotherapy, what are the options? [V2—Laddered]
    o What does Dr. Oncologist recommend and why? [V2—Laddered]

- I want to continue working if I need chemotherapy. [V1—Scribed]
  o Work occupies my mind. [V2—Laddered]
  o I work with kids, I am concerned about my immune system getting weakened by chemotherapy. [V2—Laddered]

FUTURE

- How much will chemotherapy help me? [V2—Laddered]
  o I would like to understand the benefits vs. risks of chemotherapy. [V2—Laddered]
  o I would also like to learn about recovery and side effects of chemotherapy. [V2—Laddered]
- If I end up doing a brutal kind of chemotherapy, I want to get it on a Friday to recover so I can go back to work on Monday. [V3—Checked]
- Can I get treatment somewhere closer to home? Are there any local oncologists Dr. Oncologist would recommend? [V3—Checked]
- I have a friend who will drive me up here on Fridays if necessary. My daughter is supportive. [V3—Checked]

In this example, the interviewer used the checklist topics (past, present, future) as sub-headings. Sub-headings are a good idea as they split up the content of the agenda into smaller sections. When categorizing into sub-headings, the interviewer can rely on induction (bottom-up) or deduction (top-down). Using induction, the interviewer reviews all the client issues and clusters them into categories based on internally coherent groupings and themes, with a summary label. The interviewer then rearranges the issue list so that each issue is presented under a category heading.

Conversely, when following a deductive approach, the interviewer imposes a framework and categorizes each item under the subheadings in that framework. I often use past, present, and future to categorize issues as well as prompt for them. It's a simple framework, and people often resonate with chronology as an organizing principle.

In addition to facilitating SLCT with clients, you can self-administer the SLCT process. Either way, the product is a SLCT discovery note—a written document that summarizes the client agenda.

Here is a completely generic representation of how the SLCT discovery process results in a fully documented client agenda. Let's assume the client has three issues at the tip of the iceberg, the second of which is a question. The interviewer duly captures them, without interrupting, in the scribed version of the SLCT note:

Version 1—Scribed
1. Issue 1.
2. Issue 2?
3. Issue 3.

The interviewer asks if the client has any more questions, and the client demurs. Now the interviewer asks for more detail, and the client elaborates, while the interviewer documents the laddered version:

Version 2—Laddered
1. Issue 1.
    a. Elaboration 1a.
    b. Elaboration 1b.
2. Issue 2?
    a. Elaboration 2a?
3. Issue 3.
    a. Elaboration 3a?

Next the interviewer applies a checklist, resulting in the checked version of the SLCT note. The checklist will vary depending on the domain. For example, in financial services, Wells Fargo has published Priority Cards, which serve as prompts for clients to check in on a broad range of topics. The Priority Card topics include retirement, dreams, education goals, estate planning, medical costs, and taxes. In medical diagnosis, a checklist might include a review of systems such as eyes, ears, nose, mouth, throat and so on. In medical decision making, a checklist might include diagnosis, treatment choices, and risks and benefits. Here is a generic representation of the client responses when the interviewer checks in with topics from a prompt sheet during SLCT:

Version 3—Checked
- Checklist topic 1.
   - Response 1.1.
   - Response 1.2.
- Checklist topic 2.
   - Response 2.1.

Finally, the interviewer categorizes the laddered issues into desired headings for presentation, and triages or edits for clarity and brevity. You can use any categorization scheme that makes sense for summarizing the client agenda.

Recall that one approach is to use the same categories as were used for checking. That is consistent with a deductive, or top-down, approach to categorization, sometimes called framework analysis because it uses a pre-existing framework to structure the content.

As I've mentioned previously, my favorite simple framework is past, present, and future. Chronology can be very helpful in structuring client issues because it separates those concerns we cannot control (the past) from the ones we can still influence (the future) while honoring the fact that the past and present will typically be very relevant to the future.

Do remember that an alternative approach is to infer themes from the client agenda and use those as the category headings. This is consistent with an inductive, or bottoms-up, approach to categorization sometimes called grounded theory, because the categories are grounded in the client's issues. This approach requires collecting client issues into related clusters, then adding a label that summarizes what the cluster is about.

Either way, categorizing involves merging the client issues from scribing and laddering with the client responses to the checking phase, under suitable headings.

Here, let's assume that the interviewer is going to use the chronological categorizations scheme: past, present, and future. Let's suppose the interviewer classifies Issue 3 as past, Issue 2 as future, and Issue 1 as present. Elaboration 1a turns out to be past, while Elaboration 1b is present. Elaboration 2a is future, and so is Elaboration 3a. Finally, Response 1.1 is past, Response 1.2 is present, and Response 2.1 is future.

This final discovery note summarizes the client agenda. In practice, I train people to edit the discovery note so that it fits on one letter-size page if at all possible, using bullet points. An agenda should be brief so that readers can easily skim it. This means being very terse and trusting that the client will amplify their concerns, as would be the case for any meeting agenda.

Version 4—Categorized and Triaged
PAST
- Issue 3.
- Elaboration 1a.
- Response 1.1.

PRESENT
- Issue 1.
- Elaboration 1b.
- Response 1.2.

FUTURE
- Issue 2?
- Elaboration 2a?
- Elaboration 3a?
- Response 2.1.

In brief in-person or online training, I can teach professionals to implement the SLCT process using domain-appropriate checklists and categorization frameworks. The availability of a replicable protocol like SLCT represents an opportunity to improve professional discovery of the client agenda. In my experiences to date, professionals do not yet routinely learn, as part of their training and licensing, such a client-centered approach to discovering and documenting the client agenda. I'd like to be part of redressing this deficit.

Curious about this gap in training, I reviewed the literature in financial services as part of a research report published in the Journal of Wealth Management (see bibliography). I did find some client-centered approaches to conducting discovery interviews developed by thought and practice leaders in the field.

The earliest example I could find was a book by Ken Rouse called *Putting Money in Its Place,* first published in 1986. Since then, innovators in the field have promoted a variation on financial planning known as financial life planning, which begins with discovery. Leading proponents include Mitch Anthony and George Kinder, who have written extensively about their approaches. Bob Finder has also written more generally about how financial professionals, whether life planners or otherwise, can use productive listening techniques such as "any other questions?" and "please tell me more" to surface more of the client agenda.

These thought and practice leaders are making inroads, but the professional-centered, scientific-technocratic approach to financial advising still appears entrenched.

Similarly, in medicine, my work has been inspired by patient-centered approaches to discovering the patient agenda dating back to Deborah Roter's seminal publication in 1977. This line of research stimulated other researchers to focus on discovery, including Phyllis Butow, Martin Tattersall, Richard Brown, and me.

Dozens of randomized, controlled trials in health care have shown the advantages of discovering and documenting the patient agenda, yet the professional-centered, scientific-technocratic model still predominates in health care. Medical students learn to interview patients primarily about their medical history, and discovery is anchored in this biomedical view of the patient experience.

Studies have found that SLCT generates significant increases in the quantity and quality of client disclosure in health care and, at least in early findings, in financial services as well. I will now provide more specific examples of client-centered discovery using SLCT, and contrast them with more typical professional-centered interactions.

Comparing SLCT to professional-centered discovery

SLCT corresponds to the formulate phase of the FAST process. Here is the concept map excerpt illustrating this:

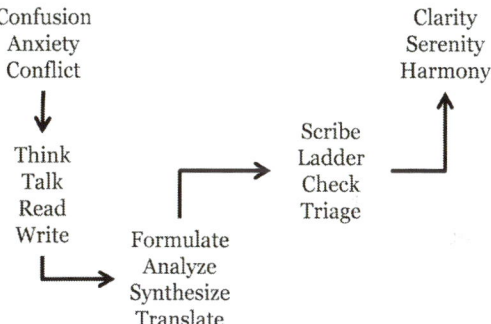

Unfortunately, professionals often ignore the formulation or discovery phase because it is too threatening. They don't really want to surface wide-ranging issues on the top of the client's mind, because they are not confident about addressing all these issues. We will see in the later chapter on leverage how issues can be addressed through referrals if they diverge too far from the professional's licensed scope of work.

In order to prevent and inhibit the real client agenda, however unconsciously, professionals implicitly skip the scribing and laddering steps. Instead, if they do any formulation or discovery at all, they jump right into checking. Often they check in with the client on the technical topics that they are most competent to address.

On one hand, this makes sense. Professionals focus on what they do best. On the other hand, it reminds me of the joke about a driver searching for car keys on the side of the road under a street lamp. A passerby asks, "Are you sure this is where you lost your keys?" And the driver says, "No, I lost them over there, but it's totally dark there. At least here I can see under the street lamp."

Professionals can waste a lot of time looking under the street lamp, when in fact the real client agenda is under the water line, to get back to the iceberg metaphor.

Here is an excerpt of a financial advisor interviewing a new client prior to being trained in SLCT. The advisor is using a standard financial discovery checklist, hoping to learn about the new client's financial condition. I've bolded those professional-centered prompts below. The problem is, the advisor leads with these prompts. The advisor will not know how much time or attention to devote to these topics without having better formulated the client agenda up front.

> Advisor: Right, so give me an idea of what your **living expenses** entail. So it's the **mortgage, property tax, medical insurance**, right?
>
> Client: Yeah… Food, prescriptions, entertainment, hair, nails, all of my bills. I went through all of my bills. My DirectTV, my Verizon wireless, my regular Verizon, my internet, my DWP, I just actually took out all of the bills and wrote down what each one was and how much.
>
> Advisor: Okay, does that include money for **travel**? Like **vacation**?

Client: I don't vacation. I don't do anything out of the norm—everything goes to the horses. I haven't taken a vacation in eight years, I consider my horse hobby my vacation. So, no it does not—I don't vacation. I don't splurge on anything—it's all about the horses.

Advisor: Wow, they're lucky to have you.

Client: They are. But you know—ya, no vacations. And I'm okay with that because I feel like I live on vacation in my house, I love my house. You know what I'm saying? When I go out to visit the horses I feel like I'm on vacation.

Advisor: Okay, so we can say your basic standard of living, really nothing extra there in terms of, I'm thinking of **vacations** or **country club memberships**, or that type of thing.

Client: No, gosh no. I have all of my car expenses, emergency car expenses all that kind of stuff, insurance, everything I could possibly think of...

This dynamic is very similar, incidentally, to the way in which physicians often begin their interviews assessing the patient's history. Here's a recent example from a clinic:

Surgeon: Okay, have you had **cancer** before and needed **biopsies**?

Patient: No. I've had all my mammograms. My mother had breast cancer when she was 55, and she had a bilateral mastectomy and reconstruction. She's fine. I mean probably 15, 18 years ago...

Surgeon: Any other **family history**?

Again, on one hand, I'm sympathetic to the idea that professionals need to know the client's financial condition, or the patient's history of cancer. My concern is that they dive in too early and too often with professional-oriented checklists. SLCT requires them to scribe (without interrupting) and ladder before checking and triaging.

Recently, I transcribed, recorded, and analyzed the discovery interviews for advisors interacting with 18 simulated clients and 12 actual clients. You can read the full account of this study in the Journal of Wealth Management. I've listed the citation details in the bibliography.

Before training these advisors in SLCT, I found that they generally led off their discovery interviews with professional-centered checklists. This had several side effects, none of them good for client-centered care.

First, the advisors tended to speak almost as much as the clients. Advisors occupied 43% of the airtime. This was in a discovery interview where they were supposed to be surfacing client questions and concerns.

Second, they asked questions in only 52% of their turns to speak. So about half the time, advisors were conversing without asking a question.

Third, when clients rated these interviews on 10 survey items, including satisfaction, the average score was 65 out of a maximum of 100.

After training, the advisors followed the SLCT protocol and began with more open-ended scribing and laddering.

As a result, they spoke less: their airtime fell from 43% to 32%. That means client disclosure time increased from 57% to 68%.

They asked questions in 67% of exchanges—around two of every three turns to speak—up from 52% or around one in every two turns.

Client ratings of the interview increased from 65 to 87 out of 100.

Let's contrast the professional-centered excerpt above with an excerpt from a SLCT interview with a different client. Notice that the advisor begins by asking if the client has written anything down for their meeting.

> Advisor: So, in getting started, do you happen to keep a list of goals or journal them?
>
> Client: Yes, I have goals that I have written down.
>
> Advisor: You do, okay. Great. And what are those goals?
>
> Client: Well, I break them into a couple of categories. I think in terms of when I would like to retire, and by that I mean that any income-generating activity I do is more for entertainment purposes or something at the margins. So I have some goals around that. I have some kind of goals around self-sufficiency. I'm a resilient sort of guy, you know, we grew up around food and I own a farm. I have some goals around resiliency, making myself more resilient. And yeah, I kind of have a number in mind—things that I feel like I need to hit so I can accomplish those goals, to leave a little bit of a legacy, you know. I don't plan on making my kids rich on my death but I would like to certainly not leave them with debt. Hopefully I can do better than that. And yeah, those are the kind of things that I have started to write down.

We can contrast this SLCT interview with the prior interview in several ways. The first interview imposed a professional-centered checklist or framework. The second opens with a question to determine what the client has been reflecting on, in writing. If the client had said "Nothing," then the advisor would have asked, "What is top of mind for you right now?" ==Either way, the advisor focuses first and foremost on eliciting the client agenda, in the client's own words and using their concepts.==

Notice that in the SLCT interview, the client specifically says, "I break them into a couple of categories." These are the client's categories, not professional categories.

Notice also that the second client does not explicitly think in terms of finances or numbers. At some point, the second client's expenditures may be relevant to the advisory relationship, but it is certainly not the starting point.

The SLCT process simply follows the client's lead. In contrast with the example just cited, other clients may not have anything written down, and they may want to start with their expenditures! As long as they are the ones driving the agenda, that is perfectly client-centered. Here is the same trained advisor speaking with a different client:

> Advisor [scribing]: So, to get started, do you or [spouse] happen to write down your goals or journal them?
>
> Client: No. No, we do not do that...
>
> Advisor [scribing]: So, I guess for you then. Feel free to chime in for [spouse] and what you think she might consider. What's top of mind for you when it comes to financial matters and otherwise?
>
> Client: Is this general, not for the long term? But just for general? Right now is just to make

sure we have enough money to do what we want to do to cover the bills. To not worry about finances. Basically, no financial worries. For us, I believe it's just having money to do what she wants to do and just not worry about not having enough to do at this time or whatever comes about. Just try to reduce the stress and worries about money.

Advisor [scribing]: Aside from finances, what other things are top of mind or side of mind for you and [Redacted]?

Client: Maybe it's not retirement at this time, but I think it's the kids. Making sure that they're getting out of high school and going in the right direction. That they're moving in the area that we want them to. Right now the kids' immediate future is what we are facing.

Advisor [laddering]: Can you say more about the immediate future?

Client: Really the short term goals are to make sure my son is getting to go to a private school. Getting the private school stuff taken care of, but also helping him get prepared for college. He needs a little extra work, and he's working really hard. We're trying to help him as much as we can. So, getting him prepared for college. Plus the other one, the middle daughter is ready to go. I don't worry about her. She's got a good plan.

Again, the client sets the agenda. This one did focus more on financial issues, but was generated by the client, not by premature use of a professional checklist.

Using SLCT with learn/earn/serve checklist

Here's another excerpt of a discovery interview I conducted with a client who was about to retire and wanted to prepare for a meeting with a retirement specialist at work. I used a particular checklist, learn/earn/serve/play/create/love, that I developed for stimulating broader client responses in financial discovery interviews.

> JB [scribing]: Okay, so my first question really is: have you already started this process by yourself? Have you made any notes, or written anything down? And if so, let's start there.
>
> Client: Okay I've written down a couple of things. I want to know if my retirement date has to be at a particular place and time—at the beginning or the end of a calendar month, or a day of a week—does it need to be a Friday rather than a Monday.
>
> JB [scribing]: Okay I'm just writing this down. Okay I got it!
>
> Client: Okay, somebody told me once that there was an advantage to picking a retirement date at the end of June, rather than... right... actually there's some language I don't understand that would be helpful if the advisor could explain to me. There's something about a separation date, and a retirement date, and they're two specifically different dates.
>
> JB [scribing]: Okay.
>
> Client: And supposedly there was an advantage if I had a... one date was the end of June, and the other date was the first of July, and I don't know—is that related to the fiscal year?

JB [scribing]: Okay, I got that typed up. Other issues?

Client: Yeah I'm also concerned about medical benefits—does my employer pay for... you know, if I retire at the end of a month, will my employer have paid for benefits for the following month?

JB [scribing]: Got it.

Client: And my last question is, basically my supervisor wants me to look into the option of returning part-time after retirement, and he gave me a PDF with a bunch of information, but it isn't really clear. It spent a lot of time talking about what happens to people who take the monthly retirement supplement, and I'm looking at doing the lump sum cash out, and I can't tell whether or not that recall process exists if you take the lump sum.

After scribing some more, I switched to laddering and asked the client to elaborate on each of the above issues in turn.

After laddering the client's initial issues, I used a divergent checklist, as a means of assuring that the client was not only focused on short-term tactical issues surrounding retirement. I invented this checklist based on an old rubric about how one should live one's life learning, earning, and serving. I added playing, creating, and loving.

The important thing about these topics is that they cover a broad spectrum of human activities. Other broad checklists could serve. Here's an excerpt from the checking section:

JB [checking]: I can run you through some other topics that kind of covers the spectrum of things people sometimes think about with regards to retirement, to see if there's anything you want to ask about, if those topics in the checklist trigger any new questions or issues for you.

— Client: What a great idea.

JB [checking]: Okay, there's six topics, and I'll read them to you and we'll go through them one at a time. The six topics are learn, earn, serve, play, create, and love. And so I'm going to go through each of those, and it's kind of like a lightning round—if you think of anything, that's great, and if not, we'll move on to the next one. So, for learning, the first one, this is really about your plans for further education for yourself, or for people around you, and if those plans have any implications for your retirement planning now.

Client: Ah, actually, that's really good. So, my learning triggers for me that I actually like to be teaching, and I have been teaching at an extension program, which is semi-tied to what I currently do—it's the same tax deduction information and whatnot—so I would love to know, will my retirement impact that particular instruction… my ability to continue doing that instructor position.

JB [scribing]: Okay. Okay, and so anything else education-related, either for yourself or for people around you?

Client: I don't think so, I'm not planning on going back to school, other than to continue, maybe even expanding my teaching—I'm actually thinking about teaching water aerobics, but that's a whole new career.

JB [checking]: Okay. Okay, and then the next category is earn, and we've talked about that a little bit, in terms of whether you can be re-hired by your current employer, even after retiring. Was there anything else related—and you've talked now about the instruction for two different kinds of teaching opportunities—was there anything else related to earnings?

Client: No, I don't think so.

JB [checking]: Or on the flip side of earnings, expenditures?

Client: Yes, sounds frightening. I'll need to get a coach on how to spend less money. Nothing really comes to mind.

JB [scribing, then checking]: Okay well I wrote that down, that might be something that triggers opportunities to get advice or coaching on budgeting. And then frequently people are thinking about service, and when we say serve we mean any kind of community service, and any way you define community.

Client: Well let's see, so I am thinking about relocating to the community I'm thinking about moving to—that one of the things I would love to do is to volunteer at two different organizations out there, one being the senior center, and the other being a cancer support group—it's more than a support group—cancer support program. And part of my desire to volunteer is of course because it's a good way to get your foot in the door in sometimes volunteer positions that are funded positions.

JB [scribing]: Okay, and I'm sort of connecting the dots in what you're saying between: you're retiring, but you will be looking for earning opportunities because you are concerned about your budget, so, on one hand, reducing the spending and increasing the income?

Client: Yes, yes, exactly right. I do not plan on sitting at home watching television all day.

JB [checking]: Okay. Okay, our next category though, is about recreation. So, play! You know, what kinds of hobbies or activities for fun do you anticipate, and do they have any implications for your planning now?

Client: Okay, so I do water aerobics on a regular basis, and I'm thinking that if I get certified to teach it, then I can actually do it without having to pay as much to do it. Although I have been told that a gym membership is the best use of money you could ever make, so I will probably continue.

JB [scribing, laddering]: So you'll continue that one way or another, but you are interested in teaching it?

Client: Haha, so I will definitely… I need to continue my swimming, and… other entertainment… Ah! Well, will probably go back to a little more photography that I used to do, and I'd like to get back to doing some more graphics work.

JB [scribing]: Okay. Okay, and if these trigger particular questions or thoughts for either this upcoming meeting or other meetings with other advisors, let me know and I'll write it down that way. Otherwise I'm just kind of keeping track.

Client: Okay, no nothing in particular really for now.

JB [checking]: Alright—and you've mentioned this already in some ways—the next category is create, so this relates to any creative outlets you have, however you define that. You mentioned photography, any other creative outlets that you want to think about now?

Client: So my major form of creativity was once collage, and I've never gotten around to dealing whether it's now possible on computers with creating collages. You used to literally cut and paste kinds of artwork, so I hope to spend a little time learning how to make the computer do this for me, because I would think you could make a more seamless, finished piece of work. So that's what I'm planning on doing.

JB [laddering]: Okay, does that relate back to education in terms of classes, or—?

Client: No I'm thinking more of the self-schooling method.

JB [scribing]: Okay.

Client: Just applying the time to actually do it.

JB [checking]: Sure. And then the last category is love. So this relates to, you know, the people, or other things you love and want to take care of or plan for in some way. Does that trigger any thoughts?

Client: Not for this particular upcoming meeting.

Here is the final discovery note that this client used as her agenda for the meeting with her employer's retirement specialist:

PAST
- Prior organization, had a "bonus month" of medical benefits? Will that be the case now?
- Have been teaching for an extension program.
- Enjoy water aerobics, used to do more photography, graphics work, collage.

PRESENT
- Confused about distinction between a separation date and a retirement date?
  - I think your separation is the last day you are in the office? Retirement date could be over a weekend?
  - Specific amount of time between separation and retirement? I don't understand it.
- Advantage if separation and/or retirement date was end of June or first of July?
- Was this advantage just about the fiscal year?
  - I'm looking at retiring August/September.
- I'm paid monthly—is my retirement tied to a month end date or beginning?
- Medical benefits? If I retire at the end of the month, are benefits paid for the following month?

- When my current coverage ceases, I want Medicare to be there right away. So need to know when my employer's coverage will stop, as opposed to the separation/retirement dates.
- If I can retire on the 10th of a month, benefits paid through the end of that month?

FUTURE

- My supervisor wants me to return part time after retirement. Information is unclear. Describes scenario for people doing monthly retirement; refers to lump sum option, but only to a restriction on being hired into a career-eligible position?
  - What are the rules if I take the lump sum cash out?
  - Could I be rehired part-time, 20 or 40%? What about a contract?
- Like to be teaching. Will my retirement affect my ability to continue existing instructor position?
- Maybe expand teaching. New career, teaching water aerobics.
  - Could be certified to teach it. That would make it more economic.
- Relocating. Volunteer at senior center; and cancer support program.
  - Sometimes volunteer positions lead to funded positions.
- Hope to spend time getting computer to make collages. Self-schooling. Take time to actually do it.
- Photography. Graphics work.

The beauty of the SLCT discovery process is that it actually requires very little effort or thinking by the interviewer. The client tells you what is at the tip of the iceberg, then elaborates, then responds to your checklist prompts. The only real effort is the discipline to stay on task with the process; and to categorize the issues so you can summarize them under headings, while editing for brevity and clarity (triage).

Measuring client-centered discovery

When I ask professionals if they are surfacing the entire client agenda, most tell me that they are doing fine in that regard. "My clients love me!" is what they say. That is a fine response to a different question. This reminds me of how Henry Kissinger apparently used to come out for briefings and ask the assembled press corps, "Does anyone have any questions for my answers?"

The question I am really asking is, do you follow SLCT or a similar process to ensure that you are surfacing the full client agenda?

The ideal answer, which I have never received, would be as follows: "I audio-record, transcribe, and analyze all my client interactions. From my quality audits, I have ascertained that in over 99% of discovery interviews, I begin by asking for the client agenda; I listen without interrupting; ask for elaboration; and then prompt the client with a divergent checklist before triaging to focus the most time on the most important issues."

Although professionals don't engage in it very often, this kind of measurement is quite feasible if you are sufficiently committed to continuous improvement. I can share with you some tools I have developed for measuring these behaviors.

One approach to measurement is by scoring transcripts. I have developed an automated way of doing this that allows me to quickly establish how well someone is following the SLCT process. I have programmed software to generate a heat map that provides a visual indication of client-centeredness.

Here is a heat map of a discovery interview conducted by an advisor trained in SLCT. I've divided the interview into the 35 exchanges that took place, featuring the advisor speaking followed by the client speaking.

The vertical axis represents the time per exchange. The dark shading shows the advisor talk time per exchange. Stacked on top of that is a lighter chart that shows how much additional time, if any, the client occupied in that exchange.

From this chart, I can quickly ascertain that the advisor spoke 27% of the time to the client's 73%. The advisor asked questions in 63% of the exchanges. The peaks represent different phases of SLCT. Initially the advisor introduces the interview and asks for top of mind issues. The client responds with some lightly-shaded peaks. Then the advisor asks for elaboration. More lightly-shaded peaks. Finally, the advisor presents a checklist, and stimulates additional lightly-shaded peaks.

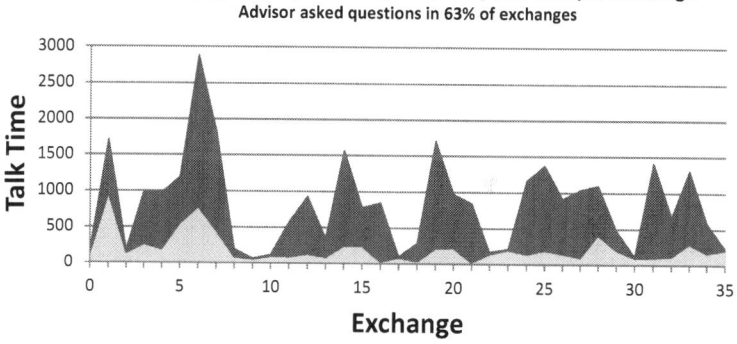

A senior executive at a company that analyzed these data said, "You can see the tall icebergs!" Indeed.

Now compare this with a discovery interview of similar length where the advisor was not trained in SLCT. Here the advisor occupied 54% compared to the client's 46%, and asked questions in only 26% of exchanges. Here the client icebergs (dark shading) are shorter and stunted and often dominated by the advisor's talk (light shading).

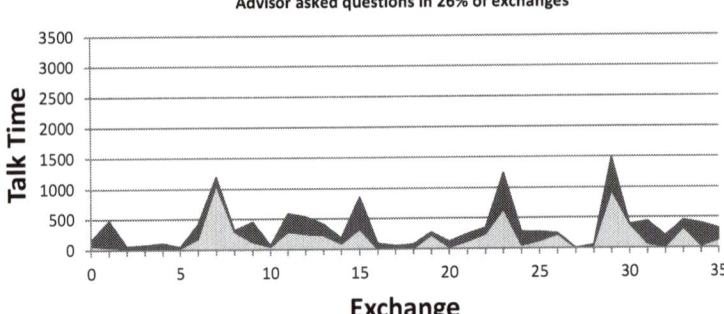

Indeed, one of the services I provide for professionals is to diagnose their discovery interviews using rigorous measurement based on transcribed audio-recordings.

Another approach is simply to ask both client and professional how they rate the interview. I created the following survey to be symmetric, meaning I can administer the same items to both parties in an interview. The survey is scored on an overall scale of 0 to 100.

Iceberg Interview Rating Scale

Please rate each of the following items on a scale of 0 to 10, where 0 means "not at all" and 10 means "fully."

1. The client disclosed important issues.
2. The client disclosed issues that were uniquely personal.
3. The client raised a broad range of issues.
4. The client disclosed sensitive issues.
5. The client explained responses in detail.
6. The interviewer listened without interrupting.
7. The interview featured enough quiet time for thinking.
8. I felt comfortable participating in the interview.
9. The interview was a positive interaction.
10. I am satisfied with the interviewer's ability to conduct interviews.

Before SLCT training, interviewers rating their own interviews tend to indicate that they see room for improvement in the client's disclosure (i.e. they did not fully elicit important, personal, wide-ranging, sensitive, detailed issues) and in the interviewer's behavior (listening without interrupting, allowing quiet time). Clients tend to be slightly more generous in rating the interviewers, but still see room for improvement. After SLCT training, interviewers and clients both rate the interviewers much closer to the maximum on each of the 10 items above.

My first customer in financial services process explained to me that they saw SLCT as the first step in a chain leading to better business outcomes for everyone.

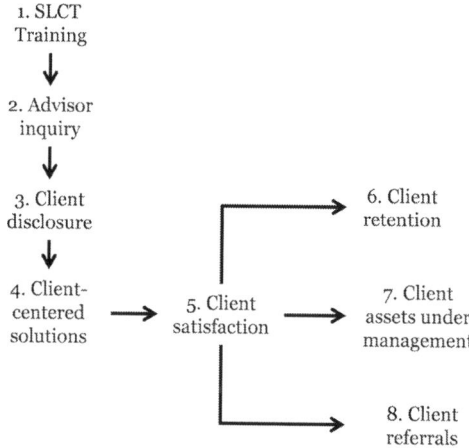

In this firm's view, shown in the numbered flowchart above, the SLCT training (1) led to improved advisory inquiry (2), and greater disclosure (3). Thanks to the deeper disclosure, they saw advisors creating more client-centered solutions (4), with an increase in client satisfaction (5). Over the medium term, they expect this increased satisfaction to directly increase client retention (6), assets under management (7), and client referrals (8). While there are many other activities that can contribute to these win/win outcomes for advisors and clients, the firm felt that better discovery was among the more important strategic initiatives they could undertake.

When this wealth advisory firm began to expand the use of SLCT, they decided to focus on referrals that were coming to them from a large brokerage firm. This brokerage does not provide a full range of wealth advisor services. When a client expresses a need for such services, the brokerage refers this client to four or five wealth advisory firms. If these wealth advisors were all equally competitive, you'd expect each of them to win the business in about 20 to 25% of the referrals.

I looked at the close rate data for the 18 months leading up to SLCT training at my early adopter firm.

The advisors we examined had a close rate of 22% before SLCT training.

In the 12 months after SLCT training, at the time of this writing, the same advisors had a close rate of 58%.

This is a small sample, and the post-training close rate will fluctuate due to the length of the sales cycle. Still, it provides some early evidence that the logic model in the flowchart above bears out in reality. Good discovery is good for everyone. Clients are better served, and reward their advisors with more business.

I will return to my experiences with this financial services firm in Chapter 7, to describe exactly how we redeployed their workforce to improve client outcomes through improved discovery. First, though, I would like to describe what to do with the patient agenda once you have surfaced the whole iceberg. This will be the topic of the next chapter, on engaging your client in decision support.

Chapter 5 concept map

In Chapter 5, I described an evidence-based way to implement the formulation phase of the FAST process with clients, which corresponds to discovering the client agenda. This method is called SLCT, pronounced "select," and the acronym stands for Scribe, Ladder, Check, and Triage. Studies from health care and financial services show that SLCT is associated with increases in patient and client satisfaction, in patient and client disclosure; and, for medical patients, reductions in anxiety, distress, decisional conflict, and regret. SLCT is valuable because it is a reproducible protocol for discovery that any professional or para-professional can master. The concept map below shows how SLCT fits into the overall flow from client confusion, anxiety, and conflict to clarity, serenity, and harmony.

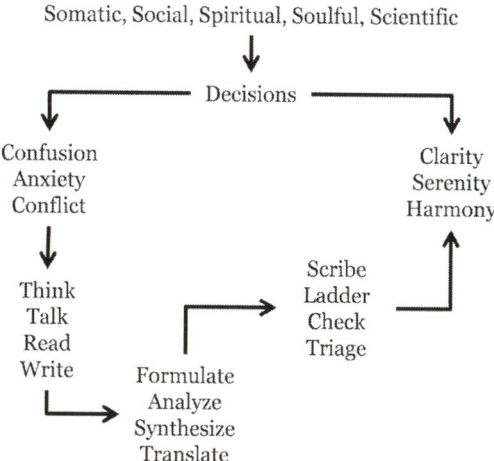

Exercises for the reader

1. Try the SLCT process with a friend or family member. Then try it with a client. If at first you don't feel confident in the checking or triaging steps, start with just scribing and laddering.
2. Practice scribing without interrupting. You will probably find it challenging, because your curiosity and enthusiasm make you want to interject, perhaps to ladder prematurely. Stay quiet. Let the client saturate their initial list before laddering. You'll find your silence serves to allow the client to self-ladder.

3. Experiment with different topics in the checking phase. Can you identify an externally-validated industry checklist that you can use?

DEAL! Recipes: Chapter 6

Engagement

*I don't always think about my decisions, but when I do…
I prefer SCOPED.*
             The Most Interesting Man in the World

When you have formulated issues using a discovery process such as SLCT, frequently you will surface a decision. In that case, recalling the FAST process from Chapter 4, the next step is to further analyze the issues, synthesize insights, and translate the insights into action. To this end, I developed a process called SCOPED to guide people to good decisions.

SCOPED stands for Situation, Choices, Objectives, People, Evaluation, and Decisions. The steps in SCOPED allow you to progressively, and sometimes iteratively, analyze issues and summarize insights leading to clarity of action. The steps are as follows:

1. Situation: clarify the key facts about your condition. This is the place to note any assumptions and questions about exactly what has happened in the past, leading up to the present.
2. Choices: clarify the options available to you.
3. Objectives: clarify your goals, in order of priority.
4. People: clarify the roles and responsibilities of the people involved in your decision. I use a framework from Bob Cronin called Voice/Vote/Visibility. Voice means you want the person to offer advice and make recommendations. Vote means you want them to make

the decision with you. Visibility means you don't want their voice or vote, but you will keep them informed so they know what's coming.

5. Evaluation: clarify the impact of your choices. One way to present the evaluation section is in a table showing how each choice (e.g. in the rows) intersects with each objective (e.g. in the columns). Then in each cell of the table, you write a brief summary of how pursuing each choice may impact the objective. Alternatively, you can cluster the evaluations under headings for each choice, or for each objective.

6. Decision: list the best choice, and next steps. When the best choice is not obvious from the evaluation, I use the five drivers from Chapter 1 as a tie-breaker. Checking in on somatic, social, spiritual, soulful, and scientific leanings can help people converge on a preferred course of action.

Here is how SCOPED fits into the concept map for this book:

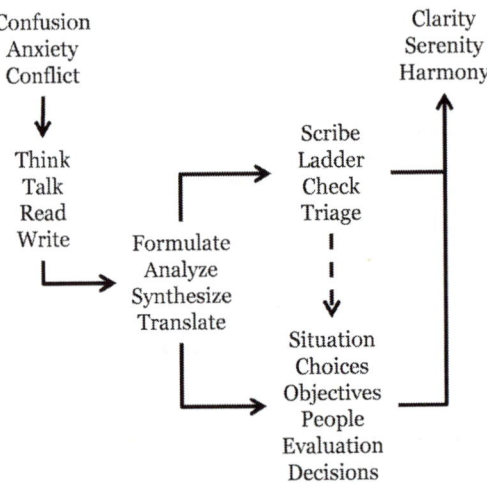

Scoping where to have lunch

One of the first times I presented SCOPED to professionals was at a conference for surgeons. The conference took place near San Francisco's Union Square. I needed a simple example to illustrate how SCOPED works. That day, the surgeons were on their own for lunch. So I taught them to scope their lunch decision. Now, I realize that this is a trivial decision. More serious examples will follow. However, the "where to have lunch" decision does illustrate the process succinctly. And, the audience liked the example because they said they often spin in circles trying to figure out where to go for lunch at conferences.

SITUATION (clarifying key facts)

- On your own for lunch. Break is from 12:30 to 1:30 pm.

CHOICES (clarifying which options are available)

- Three restaurants close by are Farallon, Postrio, and Canteen.

OBJECTIVES (clarifying goals and priorities)

- Quality and uniqueness of food; décor and service; cost.

PEOPLE (clarifying roles and responsibilities)

- Concierge—ask for recommendation.
- Colleagues—vote on restaurant after hearing recommendation and reading Zagat reviews (quoted below).

EVALUATION (clarifying impact of choices)

- Farallon: "Feels like a surreal aquarium; pampering service; exquisite, fresh seafood; especially cool for clients and out-of-towners; $45."
- Postrio: "Showy experience; knowledgeable service; Wolfgang Puck haute American cuisine; $45."

- Canteen: "20-seat, 1950s diner; minimal decor; clever Californian cuisine that matches many multi-stars without the pretension; $32."

DECISION (clarifying best choice and next steps)
- Where would you go based on the Zagat reviews?

One member of the audience wrote me years later to say he was still using SCOPED and fondly remembered his lunch at Farallon.

Scoping a treatment decision

Having assisted the surgeons in attendance with the vital lunch decision, I next showed them a medical example. The SCOPED process is identical, but this time the stakes are higher. Here a surgeon is scoping a decision for a patient regarding a precancerous condition in the breast. She wrote out the key issues and trade-offs for the patient using the SCOPED format.

SITUATION (clarifying key facts about your condition)
- You have ductal carcinoma in situ.
- In the breast are lobules where milk is produced.
- The lobules are connected to the nipple by ducts.
- There are cells lining the inside of the ducts.
- These cells have developed some cancerous types of changes.
- They are not invasive but could become cancer.

CHOICES (clarifying which choices are available)
- Active monitoring.
- Lumpectomy and radiation, plus hormone treatment if needed.
- Mastectomy, plus hormone treatment if needed.

OBJECTIVES (clarifying goals and priorities)
- Avoid recurrence as invasive cancer.
- You said you want to "keep implants."
- And that you "don't want a lot of down time."

PEOPLE (clarifying roles and responsibilities)
- Patient—this is your decision.
- Surgeon—I will make a recommendation.
- Oncologist—will discuss hormone treatment with you.
- Radiation oncologist.

EVALUATION (clarifying impact of choices)
- Active monitoring: Over 20 years, there is a 50% chance nothing would happen. But there is a 50% chance that you would develop invasive cancer.
- Lumpectomy plus radiation: Risk of invasive cancer down to 5-10%. Small possibility of damage to the implant since it's saline. Radiation can make the capsule around the implant very hard, even though the implant is behind the muscle. Not a lot of down time.
- Mastectomy: The alternative would be to remove all of the breast tissue in which case you don't need radiation. That's called a mastectomy. You can have a reconstruction.

DECISIONS (clarifying best choice and next steps)
- I recommend a lumpectomy, which we should be able to do without affecting the implants.
- Even if you have negative margins after the lumpectomy, I would still recommend that you do radiation.

SCOPED as a process for critical reflection

Before I elaborate further on the use of SCOPED, I want to contrast the SCOPED notes above with typical decision processes, or rather the absence of decision processes. This reminds me of the joke: "What do I think of the healthcare system in the United States? I think it would be nice if we had one." Likewise, most people don't even have a decision process of any sort, much less one that is effective and efficient.

My point is that many people make both lunch and medical treatment decisions without much critical reflection. We think a little, talk a little, and often neglect to do research (read), or write.
I'm happy to say this is changing. With the internet, we can now do quick research for lunch decisions (e.g. Yelp!), or travel (TripAdvisor), and in some cases medical decisions (Healthwise).

However, we still tend not to write about our decisions. Recall from Chapter 3 what happened when I asked a surgeon if he used the checklists or whiteboards that he had been trained to use. He said he kept it all in his head—and promptly lost track of who had removed a particular mass lying in front of him on a tray.

SCOPED offers a structure for thinking, talking, reading, and writing about decisions. It works well in tandem with SLCT. You formulate and discover the issues on the client agenda (divergent thinking), then converge on a decision using SCOPED.

In fact, you can integrate the use of SCOPED into the SLCT discovery process by using the SCOPED categories as prompts during the checking stage, and then presenting the SLCT discovery note under SCOPED subheadings.

You can also skip SLCT and jump straight to SCOPED if you are confident that all the key client issues are at the top of the iceberg already and there is no need to probe below the surface.

When you have drafted a SCOPED note, whether via SLCT or directly, you may find areas that are underdeveloped. Such gaps in the situation, choices, or evaluation section may highlight information sweet spots that you need to address with research (reading). Lack of clarity about objectives may lead you to think out loud (talk) or write about what is important to you. Lack of clarity about people may lead you to speak with key participants or stakeholders.

As you use SCOPED to balance your thinking, talking, reading, and writing, you should also balance the five drivers discussed in

Chapter 1. Ideally, SCOPED will clarify how you feel somatically, where you are driving socially, whether you need spiritual guidance, how to proceed soulfully, and to weigh scientifically the consequences of each choice.

On that last point, the scientific weighing of consequences: you can extend SCOPED to pursue as much quantitative analysis as you find useful. In the evaluation section, you can conduct scenario and sensitivity analyses using decision trees or Monte Carlo simulations or neural networks or the Analytic Hierarchy Process or any other method you prefer.

I urge you to remember, however, that all quantitative methods are in the service of generating insight, which is qualitative. I learned this from Pirsig's *Zen and the Art of Motorcycle Maintenance*. As I tweeted at the start of Chapter 2: Quality is qualitative. That's why it's called quality. Otherwise, it would be called quantity.

Indeed, my overall approach to critical reflection, while analytic and reductionist, honors and serves holistic drivers such as the somatic, the spiritual, and the soulful. Some historians characterize the evolution of western civilization as a conflict between Athens (seat of rationality) and Jerusalem (seat of passions and emotions). I see the relationship between reductionist and holistic approaches more in terms of a dialectic process. Analytic and holistic approaches should be able to serve each other in a virtuous spiral of insight.

Professional applications of SCOPED

In my last example, a surgeon used the SCOPED process to summarize her recommendation, as well as the reasoning behind it. This is an example of scoping decisions in the later stages of critical reflection.

Very few professionals routinely create summaries in plain language, with such a layered structure to scaffold the client's understanding. If professionals create summaries at all, they tend to be self-serving, using technical jargon and shorthand; or for the benefit of other professionals.

For example, physicians have long documented their visits for billing purposes, for legal reasons, for referrals to other physicians—in short, for everyone except the patient. This is finally changing with the advent of more lay-friendly after-visit summaries. Unfortunately, many of these after-visit summaries are generated from canned phrases stored in a database. I am actively promoting the use of SCOPED in medicine to document, in a plain-language summary written by a student intern, what specifically the doctor and patient discussed during a visit.

In addition, professionals, as well as other members of an advisory team, can also use SCOPED in earlier stages of critical reflection. In Chapter 7, I will discuss how valuable it can be for junior members of a professional team, including trainees, to facilitate SLCT and SCOPED. They can cost-effectively administer these interventions over time. This allows clients to engage in what Piaget called equilibration. Equilibration is the process by which people assimilate new information; and then accommodate or adapt their thinking to it. This requires time.

That's why I think it's a big mistake for health care systems (in the United Kingdom, for example) to adopt quality measures and incentives related to the speed at which cancer patients begin surgery. I understand that the National Health Service in the UK is trying to be patient-centered and responsive to patient complaints about delays and difficulties in accessing care.

However, anyone diagnosed with cancer, or facing any life-changing condition (change in employment, marital status, family status, and so forth) needs time to assimilate and accommodate new information. Experienced surgeons and oncologists know that they must see patients several times over a period of weeks to convey the diagnosis, and then discuss treatment options. SLCT and SCOPED can help the patient in assimilating and accommodating the diagnosis, and its options and outcomes.

Even in emergency rooms, the signs say, "This is a life or death emergency. Time is of the essence. Everybody slow down."

Another application of SCOPED in professional settings is when laypeople, or clients, self-administer the process. When I emerged from my doctoral study, I had uncovered all the ingredients I needed to coach patients to reflect critically on their treatment decisions. However, I needed to simplify the process so that patients could self-administer it, which would also make it easier for professionals or others to facilitate it.

As any good scientist would, I experimented on myself. I was facing a health-related decision and used it as a case study for developing SCOPED.

I want to share this story with you in some detail, as I think it will deepen your understanding of SCOPED, as well as the other processes and frameworks I have presented so far. I also offer this case study as a relatively ideal example of what can happen when a well-prepared client (in this case, patient) meets with a client-centered professional.

I could equally well have shared the story of any of the 3,000+ patients from my support program. The main advantage of sharing this story is that I have access to all the patient's thoughts and feelings (mine); I can share this case publicly without compromising anyone else's privacy; and it was the case that started me down the path I am on today.

Scoping my vision—personal case study

Here's the context for my personal case study. As I mentioned earlier, after completing my doctoral dissertation on the subject of medical decision making, I could not see a career path in patient advocacy. Adrift, I did what any self-respecting Stanford engineer would do. I started a software company with some friends.

Our goal was to democratize the use of decision analysis by embedding it in enterprise software. We tried selling our software to, successively, the pharmaceutical, health care, oil and gas, high tech, and banking industries. We had enough success to keep going, but not enough to find a foothold and launch the company on a solid trajectory. After four years of this, my head was spinning from all the different markets we had tested. I felt disconnected from serving a concrete need in the world.

So I took some time between jobs to plan my next career move. It also seemed like a good time to address some of my own deferred needs, one of which was my vision.

Compared to other health care needs in the world, my issues with vision were paltry and very common. I was near-sighted, and also had a distortion on my lenses known as astigmatism. I wore glasses and contacts, both of which were slightly vexing as they were uncomfortable and a hassle. I loved to play soccer and basketball, both of which required great vision and mobility, neither of which my glasses and contacts offered. My poor vision on the court contributed to a collision in which I broke my nose on a defender's head. Painful.

Again, I was fully aware that these were minor issues in the grand scheme of things. But it seemed my quality of life could be better with better vision. Tackling (and documenting) my vision decision also turned out to be a useful teaching case, because many people have less than perfect vision and can relate on some level to decision making in this area.

As a teaching case, my vision decision also works because it exemplifies many of the processes and frameworks I have presented here so far. For example, going back to Chapter 1, there were indeed several drivers forcing the issue.

I've described the somatic driver: my physical discomfort. Then there were some social drivers. I was bombarded with advertising for LASIK eye surgery popular at that time. In addition, the friends who had good experiences with LASIK raved about how great it was to get up in the middle of the night and actually be able to see.

In terms of soulful drivers, it just did not fit my self-image or identity as an athlete, as a traveler, or as a husband or father, to be hampered with glasses or contact lens paraphernalia. It also did not fit my vanity! I noticed that my wife only complimented me on my appearance when I was wearing contact lenses—but these made my eyes very dry and were really uncomfortable to wear for very long.

The soulful drivers got confusing, because neither did it fit my self-image to be vain! This in fact connected to a vaguely spiritual issue for me. I usually want to bear minor burdens mindful of the fact that my life overall has been blessed with good fortune. I usually see it as tempting fate to try to optimize on a situation like vision where I am only slightly inconvenienced. I had this superstitious feeling that God or some higher power would punish me for being ungrateful by causing the vision correction surgery to backfire and make me blind. As I wrote in a note to myself at the time, "I have a tendency to mess with success and create a 75% situation by trying to improve a 95% solution to 100% optimality."

Referring back to Chapter 2, then, I was not in the desired state of clarity, serenity, and harmony. I was experiencing some confusion and anxiety as I contemplated possible surgery.

Taking my own medicine, I realized that my anxiety was connected to the fact that I was not balancing all four strategies of critical reflection (Chapter 3). I was thinking a lot, and talking to a few friends, but had not really read much or written about anything about LASIK surgery or the alternatives.

Luckily I was patient with myself. It would have been easy to be impulsive, and resolve my confusion and anxiety by simply saying, "Just go for it! Have the surgery already!" But I knew, as described in Chapter 4, that it takes time to formulate issues and that, confronted with a complex dilemma, we laypeople will experience divergence before our analysis converges and we can synthesize insights for action.

Following the SLCT process described in Chapter 4, I eventually sat down and wrote out an initial list of issues I was facing. Here is the initial list I made in brainstorming mode:

- Can't see around the house at night.
- Hate to carry all the vision correction accessories (contacts, cases, cleaners, spares).
- I'm a hazard to myself and others driving after dark.
- Glasses are a hassle to wear during sports.
- Glasses are a hazard to wear during sports.
- Hard to find comfortable prescription sports goggles.
- Don't get compliments on my appearance when I'm wearing glasses the way I do when I'm not.

Eventually I would elaborate and then check and triage this list. First, though, to balance my writing with some reading, I went looking for some good articles about LASIK surgery. I stumbled on a great article in, of all places, *People* magazine, while I was waiting for a dentist appointment.

The article described the work of Dr. Richard Abbott at the University of California, San Francisco, who had the distinction of performing LASIK while wearing glasses himself. Here's how *People* described Abbott:

> A father of three whose wife, Cecilia, 55, a fashion consultant, has had the surgery, Abbott praises LASIK but also warns that it is irreversible, carries the risk of complications and isn't for everybody--himself included. "My glasses don't bother me," says the nearsighted Abbott. "I like perfect vision, and no one can guarantee that after the surgery."

People went on to ask Abbott what can go wrong with the surgery.

> Severe complications such as infection or irreparable problems with the flap are extremely rare. Other difficulties might include glare, halos around lights and slight double vision. In some cases these can be corrected with glasses or contacts, or improved by reoperating. But the problems may be permanent.

The article summarized Dr. Abbott's analysis of other considerations, and then concluded with his bottom line advice for people considering LASIK:

> They need to make their decision based on careful research--patients should go into it, figuratively speaking, with their eyes wide open. I get very upset when I read ads that make it seem like you're buying a new hat. This surgery is with you for life.

Having read this and a few other articles, I revisited my formulation of the issues, elaborating on my original list (that's the laddering step in SLCT) and then checking myself against the SCOPED topics as follows:

SITUATION (clarifying key facts about my condition)
- Glasses and contacts work well, but hassle, hazard, uncomfortable.

CHOICES (clarifying which options are available)
- Lasik? PRK? Intacts?
- Contacts and glasses?
- Trends? (e.g. emerging treatments?)
- Revisiting treatment later?

OBJECTIVES (clarifying goals and priorities)
- Want to avoid hassle and maintain 20/20 vision.

PEOPLE (clarifying roles and responsibilities)
- Patients like me? Eyes? Lifestyle?

EVALUATION (clarifying impact of choices)
- Side effects?
- Worst case and probability? Disaster recovery?
- Best case and probability? Typical case and probability?
- Altitude (climbing, skiing)?
- Color perception?
- Swimming?
- Flying?
- Dryness, especially indoors?
- Computer?
- Driving?
- Basketball, soccer, tennis?
- Aging?

At this point I had done plenty of thinking, reading, and writing about this decision. I needed to talk to an expert. I made an appointment to see Dr. Abbott himself.

I'm happy to say that I took my own medicine in visiting Dr. Abbott. I followed the best practices in my patient support program, which include helping patients write down their agenda (questions and concerns) prior to meeting with doctors. We also encourage and assist patients in audio-recording their visits with specialists. For ethical and legal reasons, we always obtain permission of all parties being recorded.

The idea is that patients, like all laypeople consulting professionals, need to be able to prepare for and then review the complex information and advice they receive in a consultation. This becomes an important input to the process of critical reflection, especially the analysis and synthesis phases. During these phases, being able to replay and slow down the transmission of information helps immensely with assimilation and accommodation.

So I printed out the list of questions above and brought it to the meeting with Dr. Abbott as a visual aid and memory aid. I gave him a copy as well, and with his permission, recorded our discussion.

Dr. Abbott was a masterful communicator. I'm reprinting the full transcript below, with occasional editorial comments in square parentheses.

> RA: What do you know about vision correction? [Strong opening. ==Great professionals check for understanding and diagnose gaps and knowledge deficits before launching into explanations.==]
>
> JB: What do I know about it? I basically looked at your website and sort of understood the alternatives—LASIK, PRK, of course contacts and glasses, Intacts. I understand there's new technology coming forward. So as far as the alternatives, I kind of have a picture of that. With respect to the risks, I have a little bit of anecdotal feedback, but I don't really understand... One of my goals is to understand what can really—what is the worst case scenario and what's the best case scenario in terms of treatment and treatment side effects, and then what's a sort of typical scenario.
>
> I'm curious about the recovery time and effects on things like travel. So—I don't know, does that start to tell you about where I am?
>
> RA: How old are you?
>
> JB: I'm thirty-four.

RA: (Pause.) OK. The first thing you need to understand is that any of these procedures are surgery. With surgery there are risks. Nothing is risk free. The safest option is to wear glasses, then contacts, then a surgical procedure. The surgery is quite effective. And in properly selected patients, with good surgeons and well maintained equipment, the risk for something serious happening is pretty pretty small. So you have to make sure that you are a good candidate, and that your surgeon is well trained and that the equipment is good. I think here at UCSF we are well trained, we have a lot of experience and our equipment is state of the art. With all that said, one of the key aspects of this surgery is understanding what you as a patient expect from the surgery. And what I mean by that is if you expect twenty-twenty vision and would be disappointed with anything less than that, then I would probably discourage the surgery. The idea in my mind, and I think a fair expectation, is that you have less dependency on your glasses, that in fact you may still have to wear glasses for driving at night, or for movies or plays or sporting events or to see really sharply. You may not. We may get absolutely excellent vision.

JB: Oh really? [This was the first time I had heard that I might still need glasses after LASIK. A rude awakening. I had dreamt of ditching glasses and contacts entirely.]

RA: Yeah. Now one of the things that you also need to know is that as you get into your late

30s and early forties you're going to require reading glasses. This surgery does not correct reading, and I think that's very important to know. A lot of people have the misconception that this is going to take care of everything. Now being thirty-four years old you don't have problems reading with your glasses, but as you get into your forties you'll have the option if you stay with your glasses of taking them off and reading up close without your glasses on. If you wear contacts, you will have to put reading glasses over your contacts or take them off as you get older. Especially if you're a writer and you're doing a lot of near work. This will be a reality for you in anywhere from six to ten to twelve years. There's a spectrum of age.

What's the worst thing that could happen in this surgery? The very worst thing would be loss of all vision. The chances of that happening are extraordinarily rare. We've never had that complication or close to it here. But something really bad happening is always a possibility although a very remote possibility. Most common complications or problems that people describe are: either under or over correction, so their vision is a little blurry after the surgery. Sometimes they get some astigmatism or irregularity in their vision. Some people complain of glare or halos at night—or even a little more difficulty seeing at night because of reduced contrast. Looking at your corneal map—it looks like with your degree of correction—you have a low correction with a little bit of astigmatism—that the chances of you having a good outcome are probably in the ninety percent range for close to twenty-twenty. That still means ten percent, plus or minus, that you may not achieve that. There are a couple reasons, and I think I stated that in that article, that I personally have not had the surgery. There are two main reasons. One is that my glasses don't bother me—and I can also wear contacts. And I tell my patients that if you can still wear your contacts comfortably and they don't bother you, why take any risk and have the surgery?

JB: Yeah. Well in my case I think the answer to that would be hassle.

RA: That's a lot of people. They hate the hassle of contacts.

JB: And glasses and...

RA: Right. So that's one issue and the other issue is that I am a perfectionist. I like perfect vision and I am a person that if my glasses aren't absolutely perfect or my contacts aren't perfect from a vision point of view, I bring them back and want new ones or to get them fixed. I think everyone knows their own personality and if you have a personality like that, this would not be a procedure that I would strongly recommend. Although it's excellent, nobody can guarantee you perfection. Sometimes we can go back in and touch up with a second operation to get a little closer, and sometimes we can't and that's a decision we make later. So I never want a patient to assume that "Gee, if you don't get it right the first time you can go back in and get it right the second time." Everybody is different—we're all human. The tissue all reacts a bit differently. Although the lasers are extraordinarily accurate, everybody heals a little bit differently and that's why you get a little bit of a different outcome.

The operation itself is pretty straightforward, it takes about ten to fifteen minutes to do the whole thing. I typically do one eye at a time. I do the second eye after a day or two when we've made sure the first eye is stable and looks good and you're happy and I'm happy. If there's any problem then we typically delay doing the second eye. One of my associates does both eyes at the same time, the other one does like I do, separate.

Some people complain of dryness or a little irritation after the surgery. That, I think is a real issue in about thirty percent of patients. You have to use artificial tear drops and put them in frequently for the first several months.

JB: And how about for long term, what's the percent that have to keep doing that?

RA: Probably five percent, pretty low.

JB: Oh yeah? [That number actually struck me as very high, given how much dryness bothered me with my contacts.]

RA: For a long term. The recovery is fast. You're putting some drops in for a couple weeks. You're wearing some protection when you sleep at night over your eyes for about a week. You can be back to work within a day or two. No swimming for two weeks. You can fly on an airplane within a few days of the surgery.

JB: How long do you like your patients to be nearby in terms of follow-up with you?

RA: One day, one week, usually three to six weeks, three months, six months, one year. And there's flexibility there so if someone had to go away for a six week trip, we'd just judge—plus we usually know people around the country around the world, somebody in case you had a problem. The interesting thing about LASIK, and that's the procedure that most people choose because it's the quickest recovery, less discomfort, allows us to do the second eye much quicker—is that that flap takes a good year to two years to really really heal. So if you were to get a strong blow to the eye, it could move that flap. Now I'm not talking about just a gentle touch or—but I'm talking about a real hard blow to the eye. So it's just another thing people have to consider and if contact sports—if you play basketball or tennis at the net we'd want you to wear protective eyeglasses.

JB: Huh. And if you do get a blow, are there some recovery options to go back and repair?

RA: Yeah. Yeah. We can usually repair it but not all the time. And it depends where you are and what the nature of the injury is and so forth.

JB: Yeah, it's interesting, based on what you're saying I'm not as much a perfectionist. I tend to like convenience quite a bit. So I'll compromise. Just to give you an example, I love music but I'll listen to lower fidelity recordings if it's easier to carry stuff around. A little different from the physical.

On the other hand, I don't have any problems with my glasses, any real significant problems, it's just obviously tempting, that notion of not relying on them as much, and being able to see in the middle of the night.

RA: Let me just look at one thing, at your pupil size here. Look straight ahead.

JB: That is one of the qualifications, is pupil size, isn't it?

RA: Yeah, yours are about six millimeters in a dimly lit room. So you should be fine. Although at night when your pupils dilate really widely they can sometimes get a little semblance of glare.

JB: I have now pretty poor night vision, in terms of, even with my glasses.

RA: It's not going to get better. And it may get worse.

JB: Yeah.

RA: So you need to know that up front.

JB: That's a depth perception issue, is it, or astigmatism or?

RA: No. It's a combination of different things. Can be a little astigmatism, can be just perception, pupil size, shape of your cornea. Let me take a look here.

JB: Yeah, I'd say my biggest reservations are that I experience quite a bit of dryness with contact lenses.

RA: Well, these will make your dryness worse, these surgeries.

JB: I might just be disqualified right there.

RA: There's no question. It's a little bit of a catch twenty-two, because people whose eyes are dry and are uncomfortable in their contacts will look to have a procedure where they will wear their contacts less. But we know, because we cut the corneal nerves and then we make the flap, that a full thirty percent, maybe even forty percent, have symptoms of dry eye, and those with dry eye, uncomfortable dry eyes prior to the surgery, sometime really develop significant symptoms, where they're putting drops in every hour. And that lasts typically about three months. Most of those people get better. But not all of them. And I have no way of predicting ahead of time where you'll fall. So then sometimes we have to close the tear ducts, and have to do other little things to help. So that's a real issue that you need to pay attention to if you're symptomatic of that and have had a problem with it.

JB: Well you know, maybe let's talk about some of the other strategies. Intacts—what are they?

RA: We're not doing them any more. The results were poor—poor in our hands, and they were too variable, and with your astigmatism I don't think you're a good candidate to get Intacts.

JB: What's coming down the pike in terms of the next few years?

RA: Well, we may not be operating on the cornea at all, we may be putting something inside the eye. That's one thing. Probably five to ten years. Different types of lasers. Better what we call beam profiles, a little more accuracy. Ability to customize the laser ablation to an individual cornea. Those are pretty much what's coming down the pike.

JB: And of those, the most interesting to me is not operating on the cornea but putting something inside the eye—would that be as effective in terms of astigmatism? Do you foresee limitations on that?

RA: Possibly yes. Astigmatism may be a limitation, looking at different materials, at least five to ten years.

JB: Assuming I headed down this path and things didn't go well. So I assume it's quite easy to estimate financial cost if things go typically, but then if there's need for any kind of repair or touch-up or disaster recovery of some kind—is there insurance?

RA: Well your medical insurance would control surgical problems—I think—it just depends on your insurance, you'd have to check. If you needed a touch-up, there I think the charge is now three hundred dollars. That's the least-fee charge for the laser.

JB: So in particular I need to check my insurance but in some cases they cover complications of something that they didn't cover-

RA: It's a real grey area. It's a big problem not only for our patients, but we get referred patients from other doctors, with complications. Will their insurance cover their costs here? Here, you know, if we ever had a problem we'd probably write off at least the professional fee, we would deal with it as our problem. But when it's somebody else's problem and they come here that's when it really gets difficult, and every insurance company is different.

JB: How big can the fees get?

RA: It's so rare that that happens—a typical consultation is anywhere from two hundred to four hundred dollars, the surgery could be a couple thousand.

JB: What's the impact of altitude? I do a fair amount of skiing and also mountain climbing.

RA: None.

JB: Really? I read in the Krakauer's book on—

RA: So that's RK. Different principle. That's where they weaken the cornea.

JB: Any impact on color perception?

RA: Not that I've heard of.

JB: I'm curious about—I hadn't really thought through this issue of my eyes will—I'll probably get to the point in the next ten years where I'll be reading or looking at the computer without glasses

RA: Or with reading glasses. Or taking them off. It just depends on how well you see without your glasses. We won't know that really well until you're at that age.

JB: Okay. So in a happy scenario, I can see not needing glasses for the near stuff, but I'd still need it for far stuff. So I'm using contacts that are probably—I got three boxes three years ago—are you aware of particular improvements in the contact lens technology, for especially dry eyes.

RA: Well there's new materials and new wetting solutions, it continues to improve. I don't fit lenses, so I can't tell you specifically, but I know that these are issues that are constantly being addressed. If you haven't had a consultation regarding your contacts with someone who fits a lot of these, there are new materials and there are new things out there. Make sure you have the latest.

JB: Great.

RA: Well what we'll do is I'll just have somebody come in and check the refraction. And then we'll dilate you and look at your retina, and then we'll be done.

JB: So the purpose of—you've checked my pupil size, I'm thinking of your checklist for whether I'm a qualified candidate.

RA: Well I haven't finished, I have to do a few more things.

JB: Yes, I'll be curious at the end for a summary of the dimensions of qualification and where I fall on them.

RA: Your refractive error fits within the parameters of what would be considered a reasonably good candidate. The dryness of the eye is an issue. So I'd be concerned about that. If and when you decided you were really thinking of doing it, I'd probably do a Schirmer's test, a dry-eye test to test your tear function and see what it was.

JB: Is that something we can do today?

RA: We can.

JB: Would it lead to any results that would lead me to do anything differently with respect to the contacts?

RA: No. Other than just confirm that you did or did not have dry eyes. But if you are symptomatic with irritation and feeling of dryness, to me that's more important than the test. The test is just confirmatory. Your symptomatology is more important to me. I have people who have very low tear function who are very comfortable.

JB: No, I'd be curious to do the test if it had relevance to anything else as well as this.

RA: What kind of person are you regarding your expectations? Are you more of a perfectionist type, or a little more carefree regarding what your outcome would be?

JB: I think I mentioned I'm very interested in minimizing hassle, and at the same time—the balance to me, I guess I'm sort of functionally oriented—as long as I can read, and drive. I think from an expectation point of view I'd be a pretty good candidate for this, it's just that the difference in hassle probably isn't great enough. The fact that I would be just reducing my dependence on glasses rather than getting rid of them, most likely. I don't think the difference, the gap between where I am today and where I would be in terms of hassle is big enough. Based on what I've learned, this is not something I'd try to do in January before I go on this trip. But I'm happy to have gathered some of the facts.

Even while talking with Dr. Abbott, I was converging on clarity, serenity, and harmony. However, I did not just talk and listen. I made notes as Dr. Abbott spoke. Later I reviewed my notes, and listened to parts of the recording. And then I completed the cycle of critical reflection by summarizing and synthesizing my thoughts in a written SCOPED note, shown below.

My main insights from the visit with Dr. Abbott emerged from a couple of comments he made. First, he said that the likelihood of continued dry eyes was five percent over the long term. He presented that as low. It struck me as unacceptably high. The way I looked at it, I was contemplating surgery in part because contacts made my eyes so dry. Yet there was a one in twenty chance I would have continued or even worse discomfort of this kind after surgery.

I had not appreciated that surgery would only reduce my dependence on glasses and contacts. And I had not appreciated that a blow to the head during basketball or soccer could cause major problems.

Dr. Abbott also reminded me to look more closely, so to speak, at contact lenses: "If you haven't had a consultation regarding your contacts with someone who fits a lot of these, there are new materials and there are new things out there. Make sure you have the latest." I am the one always telling patients that surgery should be a last resort, when all other less invasive options have been exhausted, yet I had not fully examined the alternative. I resolved to consult with a contact lens specialist.

Dr. Abbott's comment led me to another realization. Through some misguided frugality, I had until then always stayed within my insurance benefit for vision correction. This meant I was spending a maximum of one hundred dollars or so on eyeglasses. I could afford more, but I had allowed myself to be driven by the social structure of an insurance benefit. Like an optical illusion, this benefit made me feel like I should stay within its limit in order to maximize my value. Nonsense! Maximizing my value meant improving my quality of life, which was worth a lot more than one hundred dollars to me.

In fact, here I was contemplating 2,500 dollars in out of pocket costs on surgery, and I was constraining myself to the cheapest, heaviest, ugliest and overall worst eyeglass frames and materials out there.

The next day, I went looking for the most expensive contacts and frames I could buy.

Here is my final SCOPED note, summarizing the entire process of critical reflection, and culminating in clarity, serenity, and harmony.

SITUATION (clarifying my condition):
- I am near-sighted with astigmatism.
- I am frustrated with the hassle and discomfort associated with wearing glasses and contacts.
- My friends have had good experiences with LASIK eye surgery.

CHOICES (clarifying which options are available)
- Continue with current glasses and contacts.
- Have vision correction surgery.
- Buy better glasses and contacts.

OBJECTIVES (clarifying my goals and priorities)
- Maximize vision acuity.
- Minimize hassle and discomfort.
- Manage costs.

PEOPLE (clarifying the roles and responsibilities)
- Myself—making this decision.
- My wife and kids—have a voice in the decision, since they will be affected, for example if I go blind.
- My doctors—have a voice in the decision, as I am relying on them for professional advice.

EVALUATION (clarifying the impact of each choice)
- Objective 1 = Maximize vision acuity.
  - Glasses/contacts: 20/20.
  - LASIK: 90% chance of 20/20 vision.
  - New glasses/contacts: 20/20.
- Objective 2 = Minimize hassle/discomfort.

- Glasses/contacts: Dry eyes from contacts; headaches from glasses. Toting gear (frames, cases, lenses, solution).
- LASIK: 30-40% chance of worse short-term dryness; 5% chance of long-term dryness.
- New glasses/contacts: Finding, fitting, buying new glasses and contacts. Toting some gear.
* Objective 3 = Manage costs.
  - Glasses/contacts: $0 out of pocket.
  - LASIK: $2,500.
  - Fancy new glasses/contacts: $275 up front plus $150/year.

DECISIONS (clarifying best choices and next steps)

* Buy titanium-framed glasses and order disposable contacts from 1800contacts.com.

As my SCOPED note indicates, I ended up purchasing titanium-framed rimless glasses that weighed nothing at all and new astigmatism-correcting daily disposable contact lenses. The difference was astonishing. It was eye-opening! I never looked back! Enough with the puns already. In fact, the new contacts were so comfortable, I now wear them exclusively. No need for glasses at all.

Before we leave this case study, I want you to contrast my SCOPED note summary with Dr. Abbott's professional note, which he entered into my chart but did not give me until I requested it. I had trouble deciphering it so consider this an approximation of what he wrote:

> History of present illness:
>
> SCL wearer q t / wk disposable doesn't tolerate
> lenses very well. Exploring refractive options.
>
> 1. Inconvenience of glasses.
>
> 2. Eyes are dry.

Assessment/Plan:

Long discussion w/pt re r/b/alt/co?

All questions answered or referred.

Discuss dry eye and sx's. Pt very symptomatic.

Discuss expectations/questions.

Interested "minimizing hassle."

Discuss glare, halos, night vision.

Would recommend no surgery based on discussion with pt.

To document our interaction, Dr. Abbott was using a variation on a medical schema for documentation called the SOAP note. SOAP stands for Subjective, Objective, Assessment, Plan. This framework came of age in an era of medical paternalism when patients were not invited to be part of decision making. Subjective refers to the patient's view of what is wrong. Objective refers to the results of clinical tests (supposedly objective, in reality very much subject to interpretation.) Assessment refers to the clinician's diagnosis of what is going on. Plan refers to what the clinician is ordering the patient to do. Doctor's orders! I am promoting my SCOPED note as a 21st century successor to the SOAP note.

In comparing my note to Dr. Abbott's, the first difference is that his is shorter and contains many technical abbreviations. Another difference is that my note contains a summary of the trade-offs between the options, listed under the evaluation section. It explicitly evaluates each option according to my stated objectives. I think it's fair to say that his note is a professional note intended for other professionals (medical, legal, billing), whereas mine is specifically designed for laypeople.

Guiding people to good decisions

My experience with Dr. Abbott changed my life in several ways. First, my quality of life improved because he pointed me to better contact lenses as a good solution.

Second, I consciously used all the disparate tools and techniques I had developed as part of my PhD dissertation work, and as an advisor to Laura Esserman during my time in the world of high tech startups. Prior to this, I had studied parts of the process: for example, discovering the patient agenda; or helping patients arrive at decisions. This was the first time I had strung the whole process of critical reflection together, from formulating issues to analyzing them to synthesizing insight and translating the insights into action.

For the first time, I had a blueprint for implementing a comprehensive program of patient or client-centered care: from discovery to engagement. I could now see a career path in patient advocacy, where I had not seen it before. I would still need to figure out a crucial piece of the puzzle, one that Laura Esserman would once again provide. I needed leverage, the topic of the next chapter.

With a leveraged workforce of student interns, my patient support program now helps over 400 newly diagnosed patients a year SCOPE their treatment decisions with their surgeons and oncologists at UCSF. Earlier in this chapter I showed you one of the several thousand SCOPED notes that have helped our patients gain clarity, serenity, and harmony—as one of these patients, Mary, described so vividly in Chapter 2.

Now SCOPED has spread around the country thanks to adoption by the Cancer Support Community, and is spreading abroad through collaborations in the UK and continental Europe. It has been a dream come true for me to contribute to patient-centered care using SCOPED to improve critical reflection. And it all started with my own LASIK decision and deliberations with Dr. Abbott.

As I'll describe in more detail in the next chapter, colleagues are now taking up SLCT and SCOPED in the financial services industry.

I look forward to exploring how portable these tools may be to other professions. As a brief illustration of this portability, I want to share an example of a financial services client facing a decision about an investment her family made in a restaurant. The content is different but the process is the same as in health care decisions.

Financial services example

I spoke to Michelle as part of a training program I was developing for the financial services industry. Michelle was confused, anxious, and conflicted about whether to sell her family's restaurant, and if so, when.

I used the SLCT protocol to help Michelle formulate the issues and surface the full iceberg. I used SCOPED during the checking and categorizing phases of SLCT to check the iceberg for breadth, and to summarize and categorize her agenda. Finally, I triaged the SCOPED note so it fit on one letter-sized sheet of paper.

Before we got started, I asked to what extent Michelle had been thinking, talking, reading, and writing. Like most people, she reported that she had thought a lot, and talked with her husband, but not done much reading (research) or writing.

I also asked Michelle to rate on a scale of 0-100 where she was in terms of clarity (knowing what to do), serenity (confidence in her decision process), and harmony (alignment of resources needed to move forward). She rated clarity at about 50, serenity at about 20, and harmony at about 50.

Here's the initial list of issues Michelle shared that were at the top of her mind, or tip of the iceberg.

Version 1—Scribed

1. Opened very small restaurant in rural area.
2. Burden. Hard to hire help. Husband working seven days a week, 12-14 hours.
3. Draining for our family.

4. Don't want to quit or give up (ego) but that might be best decision.
5. I have another full-time job so can't always help my husband out.
6. We live an hour away.
7. Restaurant has been busy. We like the area and people. But tradeoff might be too much.
8. I wanted to support my husband in pursuing his standards. Thought it would be easier to find other employees who would also work to his standards. Key person bailed out.
9. First full blown restaurant. Space had limitations. We had done cost analyses, enough seats. Other limitations came into play. Size of kitchen and path, kitchen capacity for prep and volume.
10. I considered restaurant to be a financial investment. Invested some of my savings. It's my financial plan right now. Restaurant has not paid back all the investment (maybe if we sold off assets).
11. I would like to pass it on rather than just close it. Want to make money back.
12. Considerations: financial, ego, support husband.
13. My husband now has options and connections he didn't have before.
14. Meanwhile my career going better than I expected two years ago. Supporting myself and my interests.
15. Also I've learned I don't want to be managing a restaurant. Not my career path.
16. I want to support husband but balance my own needs.
17. I've been working full time, and coming in on weekends to restaurant. But my personal life has suffered—my relationships with parents, sister—need to get back in balance.

I scribed all these issues without interrupting Michelle. Whenever she ran out of steam, I asked her if anything else came to mind and gave her some quiet time to think. Eventually she had saturated all the issues at the top of her mind. I did not need to ladder very much because her thinking was so concrete.

I then used the SCOPED framework to help broaden her thinking, and we emerged with the SCOPED note below after laddering, categorizing, checking, and triaging. Michelle had entered the discussion feeling conflicted—not wanting to be in the restaurant business any more, but also not wanting to be perceived as quitting; wanting to support her husband; and wanting to make back some of the money she'd invested.

She emerged with a key insight that it was her turn to focus on herself, after supporting her husband in this venture for a few years. Also, she did not want to keep the restaurant open more than another three months due to the impact it was having on her husband's health and her quality of life.

Michelle therefore succeeded in substantially narrowing the range of decision-making. The choices now came down to either closing the restaurant in two weeks, so they could focus on selling the business; or keeping it open for three months while also trying to sell it.

I ran her through the five drivers, and overall she was leaning toward keeping it open for three months while trying to sell it. She felt herself leaning this way somatically, socially, soulfully, and scientifically.

Scoping Michelle's restaurant decision
SITUATION (clarifying key facts)
- In the middle of a lease for our first full-blown small restaurant in a rural area.
- Burden. Concerned about our health. Need a break.
- I have another full-time job so help my husband on weekends. Hard to hire help.

- My personal life has suffered—my relationships with parents, sister.
- I went in to this to support my husband in pursuing his standards. Thought it would be easier to find other employees who would also work to his standards. Key person bailed out.
- My husband now has options and connections he didn't have before.
- For these reasons, I would like to rule out keeping the restaurant.
    - We can't go on running it ourselves more than another three months without unacceptably damaging our quality of life.
    - We won't be able to find anyone to run it for us.
- Meanwhile my career going better than I expected two years ago. I focused on my husband for the last two years, now I want time for my quality of life and interests.

CHOICES (clarifying which options are available)
- Keep the restaurant open for three months while we negotiate lease and package the business for sale. Sell the assets if no buyer.
- Close the restaurant in two weeks and then negotiate lease and package the business for sale.

OBJECTIVES (clarifying goals and priorities)
- Support my quality of life (e.g. time for people) and my career (e.g. explore new directions).
- Support my husband and his quality of life (including health).
- Make back the money invested, including gift from in-laws (using it responsibly).

PEOPLE (clarifying roles and responsibilities)
- Vote: my husband and I.
- Voice: business advisor; realtor—would broker sale of the business; property owner (influence).
- Visibility: employees; husband's parents gave him some money—gift. Customers.

EVALUATION (clarifying impact of choices)
- Keep the restaurant open for three months while we negotiate lease and package the business for sale. Sell the assets if no buyer.
    - My quality of life: OK if two employees stay on. Will need to give them a week or two off from work.
    - Husband quality of life: OK but not great. No drastic impact on health over next 1-2 months.
    - Financial impact: some more revenue over next three months. Cover about half of money invested. Not sure about impact on lease? Could buy out the lease (three more years). Could perhaps negotiate our way out of it?
- Close the restaurant in two weeks then negotiate lease and package the business for sale.
    - My quality of life: better. Not serving customers.
    - Husband quality of life: Same.
    - Financial impact: would being closed affect our ability to find a buyer and negotiate the lease?

DECISIONS (clarifying best choice and next steps)
- Somatic—Gut feeling is three month option. Could feel OK about shorter timeline if husband did.
- Social—two weeks would feel abrupt for our community.
- Soulful—self-image of not giving up.

- Spiritual—does not apply.
- Scientific: rational thing is to stay open and show profit. More appealing to buy a restaurant up and running than one that closed its doors.
- Next steps: Talk to husband, business consultant, realtor.

After emailing this SCOPED note to Michelle, I asked her to rate again, on a scale of 0-100, her clarity, serenity, and harmony. Her clarity had risen to 90 (from 50); her serenity to 70 (from 20); and her sense of harmony in moving forward to 80 (from 50). She still had tasks to complete before arriving at a final decision, but she had made tremendous progress through the simple act of critical reflection using SLCT and SCOPED.

Protocol for scoping client decisions

Here is a summary of my protocol for scoping client decisions, based on SLCT discovery of the client agenda.

1. Assess degree of client confusion, anxiety, and conflict; or conversely, degree of clarity, serenity, and harmony.
2. Ask client to describe the influence of each of the five drivers: somatic, social, spiritual, soulful, and scientific.
3. Ask client about their mix of thinking, talking, reading, and writing. Ask them to read any written notes to you, or (if no written notes), to think out loud.
4. Scribe and ladder the client agenda, as described in Chapter 5.
5. Prompt the client with the SCOPED topics during the checking phase of SLCT.
6. Categorize and triage your scribed, laddered and checked notes into the SCOPED categories.
7. Give the client the SCOPED note to review and further edit.

8. Assess the degree to which the five drivers are compelling the client to clarity, serenity, and harmony.
9. Repeat the SLCT and SCOPED process if the client has synthesized new insights leading to a reformulation of the issues.

On the rare occasions when you are confident that the client has already surfaced the full iceberg of their agenda, you can skip from step 2 to step 5 in the progression above. My experience is that this direct administration of SCOPED usually results in new insights that lead the client to reformulate the issues. At that point you should follow steps 3 and 4 and proceed with the full protocol.

Chapter 6 concept map

I have positioned SLCT as a tool professionals can use for discovery, while SCOPED is intended for engaging in decision support. This separation is a little over-simplified. In practice, if you can discern in advance that your client is facing a decision, you may want to use SCOPED during the checking and categorizing phase of SLCT. This will generate a draft SCOPED note, which you can then use as the basis for further information-gathering, and eventually to converge on a decision.

Indeed, in this chapter, I demonstrated how to extend the process of critical reflection past the point of discovery, past the point of information-gathering, and on to decision making. In practice, this just means further iterations and revisions of the SCOPED note produced in discovery.

As the client finds answers to questions, the SCOPED note converges on a summary or synthesis of the thinking, talking, and reading. The client is ready to arrive at a decision. When necessary, professionals can then use the five drivers to arrive at the best choice in terms of somatic, social, spiritual, soulful and scientific signals.

The concept map below shows how SCOPED can extend SLCT, or function on its own, to structure critical reflection on the path to clarity, serenity, and harmony.

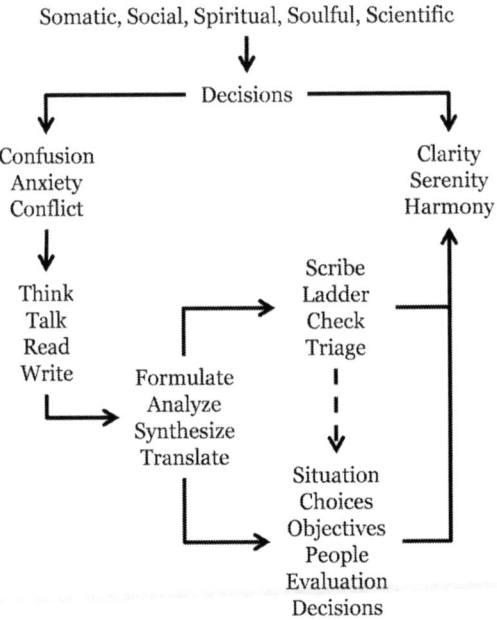

Exercises for the reader

1. To build confidence in using SCOPED, begin by scoping a relatively straightforward decision of your own, something like the example I provided on where to go to lunch.
2. Then scope a more challenging personal decision.
3. Progress to scoping a decision for a friend or family member.
4. Then try with an existing client.
5. After sufficient practice, you can scope decisions for new clients.

DEAL! Recipes: Chapter 7

Leverage

Give me a place to stand, and a lever long enough, and I will move the world.

Archimedes

You've seen how SLCT (Chapter 5) and SCOPED (Chapter 6) can structure your thinking, talking, reading, and writing (Chapter 3) and lead to clarity, serenity, and harmony (Chapter 2). You and your colleagues can use these tools to guide your clients as you formulate and analyze issues, synthesize insights, and translate the insights into action (Chapter 4). However, discovering the client agenda and engaging in decision support are time-consuming activities for professionals. This raises the question of exactly who on a client-facing team should administer SLCT discovery interviews and the SCOPED decision process?

One logical answer is that professionals are well-suited to discovery and decision support. After all, you know your clients, and know how to work with clients.

However, as professionals, you also face barriers to effective discovery and decision support—even those of you who assure me you "do this all the time." First, as experts, ==you often suffer from the curse of knowledge==. In discovery, you can't resist interrupting to answer questions rather than stay focused on eliciting the client agenda. In decision support, ==you are often tempted to be directive==.

Second, not all professionals show a strong aptitude for studying and improving their communication processes. You tend to think you are good communicators simply because you communicate with clients a lot. Sadly, people don't get better at something just because they do it a lot. They get better when they do it a lot and reflect on it a lot, and experiment with their techniques in a continual drive for improvement. This takes time, effort, and money, which many professionals prefer to invest elsewhere.

When I launched a patient support program at UCSF, I was realistic about the prospects of training our surgeons and oncologists to administer my tools to their patients. As one of my new colleagues told me, "We're not paid to talk to patients or educate them." (Conversely, a senior executive at a major financial advisory firm recently told me, "I have 10,000 advisors who are paid to talk to clients.") Times are changing in health care, and today I'm more hopeful about spreading this work among health care professionals. But at that time, I wanted to routinely implement patient-centered discovery and engagement more deeply than had ever been attempted before.

As a newcomer and outsider, I had no standing to ask surgeons and oncologists to make wholesale changes in their practices, especially since I had no resources under my control. My physician colleagues were already going out on a limb to simply tolerate my program.

Only at a patient-centered medical center like UCSF could I have successfully asked surgeons and oncologists to allow my program to operate. Keep in mind, I wanted to contact patients in advance of upcoming appointments; send them educational materials; and help them list questions, make notes, and routinely audio-record their discussions. This was already a big ask. Most physicians would have seen what I just described as unacceptable interference with their patients.

I did have a strong evidence base behind my proposed program. In addition to my dissertation research, I could rely on evidence from dozens of randomized clinical trials involving thousands of patients. These trials separately tested the components of my proposed program: sending educational materials known as decision aids;

listing questions; taking notes; making recordings; and providing decision support for patients with cancer and other life-threatening conditions.

When compared to usual care, these materials and services increased patient knowledge, question-asking, information recall, and satisfaction. They also reduced decisional conflict, anxiety, distress, and regret. They worked because they increased patient capacity to think, talk, read, and write about their diagnosis and treatment options. In other words, they helped patients to reflect critically with their health care professionals.

Unfortunately, then as now, there was no funding mechanism or business model to finance patient education as a focus of health care delivery. Like many medical centers, ours did fund a stand-alone resource center where especially motivated patients could access educational materials and get support. Such resource centers are often under-utilized because patients faced with a complex diagnosis are in overload. They often don't register the fact that there is a resource center; or they hear about it and can't muster the energy to visit.

I wanted to integrate full service patient education and engagement into the routine delivery of clinical care, rather than ask patients to self-refer to a resource center.

Doing this was going to require a workforce. Contacting patients, sending them educational materials, and providing health coaching services—all these activities require a human touch.

Laura Esserman was eager to champion our program and demonstrate its potential in the breast cancer clinic that she directed. We both knew the breast cancer clinic was an ideal proving ground: each year over 600 newly diagnosed patients came to discuss treatment options and outcomes with four surgeons and 12 medical oncologists. The treatments they faced included surgery, reconstruction, radiation therapy, chemotherapy, and hormone therapy, among others. As with all patients (and clients), they needed to balance the risks of under-treatment and over-treatment, relative to their diagnosis and personal priorities. The need for patient education was very high.

It just was not obvious to us who was going to facilitate the delivery of our educational materials and services. We tried training the clinic schedulers to send our educational materials and to offer services when patients were calling to make appointments. This was the ideal time to intervene. However, our clinic schedulers were already stretched beyond capacity, and we could not add more to their plates.

At this point, Laura had another aha moment that changed the course of my career. The first had been when she recognized the need for better discovery and documentation of the patient agenda. Now she turned to me and said, "The interns can do it."

Student intern workforce: leverage in health care

Laura was referring to a student internship program in the breast cancer clinic. As with many organizations, the UCSF Breast Care Center offers recent college graduates the opportunity to gain experience while working a few years after college, before going on to graduate school. The student interns earn a stipend acting as research or program assistants, working on studies or quality improvement projects. This is a highly competitive internship program, with hundreds of applicants each year from top universities and colleges, all vying for a dozen or so slots.

Laura and I convinced the other faculty at the Breast Care Center to let us deploy the student interns part-time as patient advocates. The interns would have the opportunity to interact and counsel patients in a way that few premedical students ever can. Our faculty agreed to lend each of their interns to my program for one day a week.

This has turned into a win/win/win situation, because this job enrichment program also has enriched our applicant pool. Every year more applicants compete for a position in this unique program. We select increasingly productive and high performing student interns for the overall internship program, which leads to productivity gains across the board. Meanwhile, patients obtain valuable support services, and students gain valuable experience.

I will now describe how this program has evolved as a case study in leveraging a junior workforce for client-centered care in a professional setting. Laura and I obtained external funding for planning and evaluating our innovation from public and private sources, most notably a Center of Excellence grant from the Congressionally Directed Medical Research Program; an innovation grant from the Arthur Vining Davis Foundations; and a demonstration site grant from the Informed Medical Decisions Foundation.

Designing for leverage: a case study

My study of systems engineering at Stanford gave me a thorough grounding in user-centered design. As I contemplated how to implement a comprehensive patient support program, it was clear that I needed to start with a picture of the patient journey, which I drew as follows:

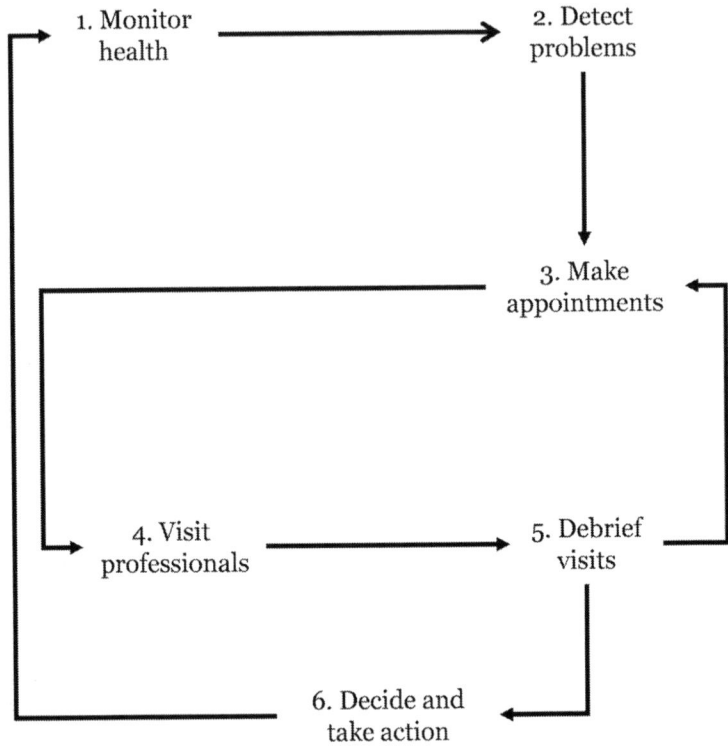

From a patient's perspective, our journey through health care begins outside the delivery system. Ideally, each of us monitors our own individual or family health with some vigilance (item 1 on my map of the journey). In practice, how well we perform this task varies from person to person and family to family, and may depend on education and other resources.

At various points in our lives, we are all going to detect a problem (item 2). Again, there's some variation here, as some of us may try to ignore problems, but eventually, we should enter the health care system by making an appointment to see a professional (3). After some waiting time, we visit the professional (4).

Afterwards, we debrief our visit with family or friends or other professionals (5). Often, the first professional refers us to additional professionals. I call this the visit cycle, like the spin cycle in a clothes dryer. We make additional appointments (back to 3).

Eventually, we explicitly or implicitly decide and take action (6), and then return to monitoring our health (back to 1).

I just used the words explicitly or implicitly to characterize patient decision making. This is because many patients (and consumers in general) end up being socially driven by professional institutions to follow train tracks that have been laid over years of paternalistic practice. They take action without realizing that they even have a choice.

I drew this picture for our clinic in particular, but my experience suggests that you may find it relevant to your professional environment as well. Please think of analogies to your world as you read this.

The next step in mapping the patient journey was to incorporate the existing supportive services in the ecosystem. I wanted to make sure we designed with the whole ecosystem in mind. A common trap in designing new programs is to ignore other offerings to clients. In practice, you need to coordinate with those other offerings so that the totality remains client-centered.

Our medical center offers many other services relevant to the patient journey. I overlaid them on my map of the patient journey as follows.

First, we conduct screening programs to help patients monitor their health (item 1a on the second map). Next, we provide navigation services to ensure that patients who have problems are navigated into the system for treatment (2a). For diagnoses such as cancer, we offer emotional support (3a) in the form of support groups or available one-on-one counseling, both with professionals and peers (the buddy system). I have not seen other professions make peer support available to the extent that the medical profession does. Food for thought.

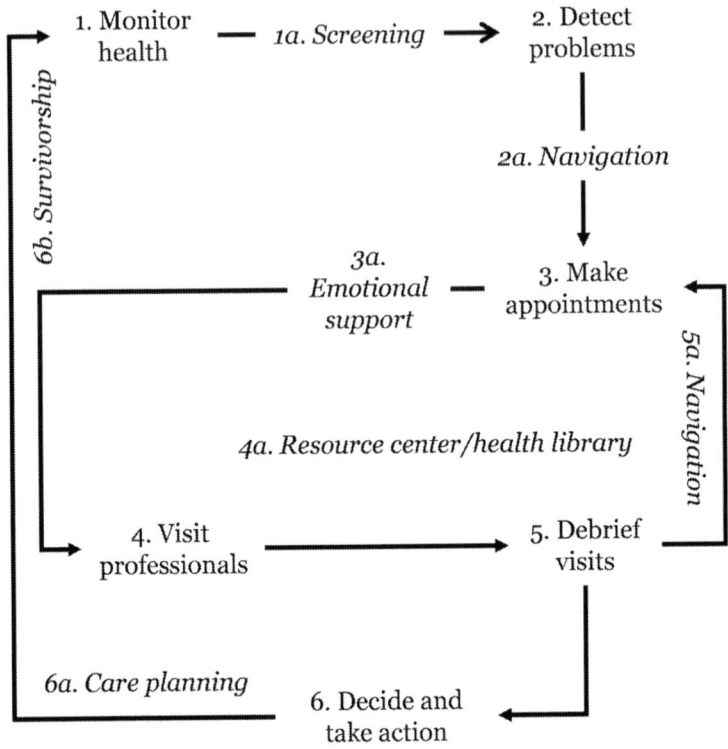

After some waiting, our patients go to their appointments with designated professionals, including physicians, nurses, social workers, psychologists and others. These visits often generate referrals to our resource center or health library (4a) as well as to other professionals, which can require additional navigation (5a). Out of a multitude of professional opinions and recommendations, our patients are expected to arrive at a coherent treatment strategy. Once a strategy emerges, our physicians and nurses create a care plan (6a) to get the patient through treatment. After treatment, patients ideally obtain a survivorship plan for getting back to a new normal, including monitoring and screening activities to detect any recurrence (6b).

Having mapped the patient journey, I perceived a few touch points where we could leverage our scarce but powerful resources for discovery and engagement. It seemed obvious that the time patients spent waiting for an appointment could be productively filled with preparation. In addition, there was little support for the actual visit.

I knew from patient interviews during my doctoral research that patients had three key needs related to information, communication, and decision making at doctor visits. First, they said they were scared by their diagnosis and needed a general orientation before going to see specialists about their treatment options. Left to their own devices, they were subject to too much, too little, or conflicting information from family, friends, neighbors, and the internet. Surveys and other research also showed that patients wanted to get this orienting information from their physicians, whom they trusted more than other interested parties such as insurance and pharmaceutical companies.

The second key need related to the fact that patients told me they would "freeze up" and forget to ask key questions when they did finally get in to see the surgeon or oncologist—even questions that had been keeping them awake at night for weeks!

The third need was that even when specialists addressed patient questions, the information went in one ear and out the other.

Based on my understanding of these needs, and map of the patient journey, I was able to design the following blueprint for providing educational materials and services to our patients.

The key patient tasks are highlighted in boxes on the last flowchart. Please note, I did not initially express these as needs, or as services to provide for patients. I wanted to indicate what prepared patients were doing, and what all patients ideally would be doing, to become as informed and involved as possible in their treatment decisions.

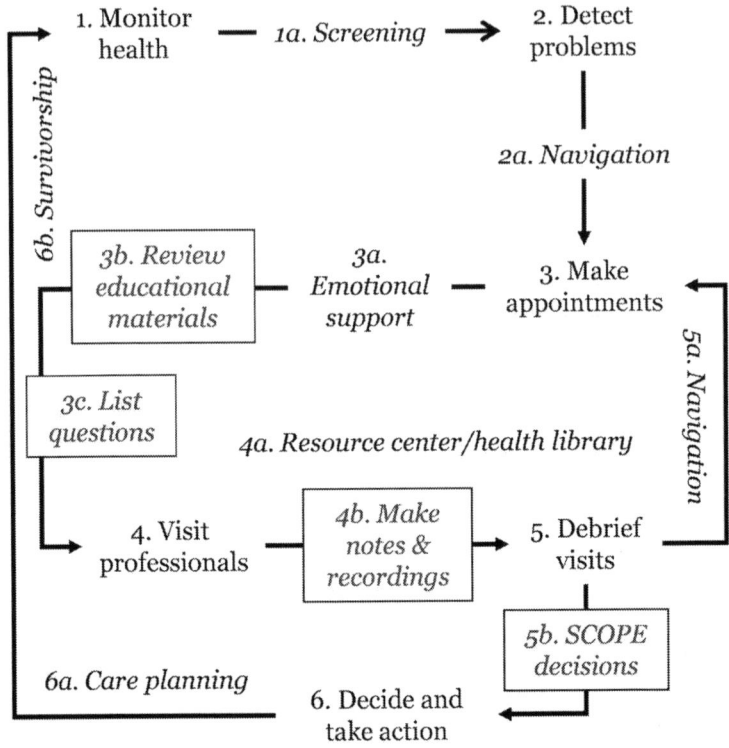

First, as soon as they had a confirmed diagnosis and a confirmed appointment, I wanted them to review good educational materials (item 3b on the revised map of the patient journey). Second, I did not want them to view these educational materials as providing definitive answers. Rather, I wanted patients to review these materials with an eye to listing their questions and concerns (3c).

I was inspired in this insight by a sign posted at the Community Breast Health Project in Palo Alto, where I had volunteered and begun my dissertation research. I mentioned this in Chapter 4 and it bears repeating:

> We have not succeeded in answering all your questions. The answers we have found only serve to raise a whole new set of questions. In some ways we feel we are as confused as ever,

but we believe we are confused on a higher
level, and about more important things.

That sign perfectly captured my conviction that critical reflection is a longitudinal process that proceeds toward insight in fits and starts.

Positioning our educational materials as stimulating questions rather than answering them also offered some important protections. First, we wanted to make it clear that these were background materials to prepare for a visit with a licensed professional. Only that licensed professional was qualified to give advice and direct care. This approach paid due respect to our professionals, who understood that we were not trying to usurp their role or undermine their expertise. Our professionals were then more tolerant than they otherwise would have been of the inevitable variations and errors of omission in packaged educational materials.

Having reviewed materials, and listed questions, the next patient tasks included asking questions, and making notes and recordings of the information and advice provided by the professional (4b). Notes and recordings are proven to increase information recall.

Finally, I wanted patients to be able to scope their decisions (5b), meaning to use SCOPED or a similar framework to evaluate the impact of their treatment options and choose on the basis of valid information and well-considered preferences.

I was fully aware that patients and families were not all able to self-administer these tasks. A cancer diagnosis comes as a shock to the system, and patients and families are sent reeling. Just at a time when they most need their coping skills, their emotions are under siege—in ways that narrow a person's usual repertoire.

Laura's key insight unlocked the door to giving patients the help they needed, though. I was able to train student interns to facilitate the completion of these patient tasks.

For example, I didn't want patients to have to come to a resource center or health library to review educational materials. So, with the assistance of my deputy and co-conspirator, Shelley Volz, we trained our interns to call every patient, identify what materials they needed, and send them out by mail or email.

We also trained the interns to coach patients in the use of our recommended strategies for becoming as informed and involved as possible. We learned that we needed to explicitly request that patients make a list of questions and give a copy to their physician at the start of the appointment. Otherwise patients were too shy to show their list to the doctor, who would remain ignorant of the overall patient agenda until his or her proverbial hand was on the clinic door.

The interns encouraged patients to make recordings, borrowing recorders if necessary from our clinic or resource center. Interns also ascertained whether patients were bringing a note-taker, and whether they needed help with language interpretation.

Along the way, we trained interns to note any barriers the patients were facing that could impede becoming informed and involved in their treatment decisions. Interns noted whether patients were coming alone; were very distressed; faced cognitive difficulties in processing information; or faced language or other barriers to communication. We trained them to recognize exceptions and escalate or refer patients to appropriate resources. I like to say that my entire role as director of this program can be summarized in two words: handling exceptions. Parenthetically, I have concluded that leaders must build slack into their schedules to anticipate the weekly exceptions that will escalate up to them.

For those patients who displayed or expressed barriers to self-administering our strategies, we had the interns offer themselves as personal health coaches. For our highest-need patients, interns made themselves available to write down the patient's questions and concerns, and to accompany the patient to the appointment to make notes and audio-recordings. Then they write up a SCOPED note so the patient can scope their options and outcomes while deliberating with family or other professionals.

In addition to leveraging our student intern workforce, we also leveraged technology. We had very little funding, and necessity was indeed the mother of invention. We were early and enthusiastic adopters of a web-based relational analytic database that we used as a customer relationship management system. We used voice over internet telephony to drive down telephone costs, and used tablet computers and digital audiorecorders to make notes and recordings. We conducted case review meetings by screen-sharing. More recently, we moved our training online so that we can be more efficient in that as well.

Eventually our initial sources of external funding expired, even as we wanted to grow outside of the breast cancer clinic. This led us to find an even more cost effective workforce. In addition to paying post-baccalaureate interns, we added college students who earned academic credit for working one day a week in our program. I am now even recruiting high school students. These are not ready to serve as health coaches, but can help our college and post-bac interns with clerical and other tasks. What I'm saying is, even my interns have interns! Now *that* is leverage!

Incidentally, patients sometimes marvel at the youthful age of my program staff when they meet in person after various telephone and email interactions. When you think about it, though, college students or recent college graduates are ideally suited to our program's forms of patient engagement.

We need a workforce able to identify high quality online materials to send patients. This is the kind of research that good students do all the time as part of a modern college education. We need a workforce skilled at formulating questions. Again, this is what good students are trained to do. We need staff able to paraphrase and summarize complex information—fast. Check. And most of all, we need trainees open to new ways of conducting discovery, such as SLCT, and decision support, such as SCOPED. Unburdened by competing frameworks, my interns learn SLCT and SCOPED faster than any professionals I have ever trained.

My colleagues and I have published dozens of scholarly journal articles describing the impact of our program. These studies show that our program is indeed associated with improved patient information-processing, communication, and decision-making. Other studies have shown that informed and involved patients not only experience better care, but also have better psychological and in some cases physical health outcomes.

We continue to struggle with funding for this program. Patient education is still considered a "nice to have" not a "have to have" overall. I understand that there are many other competing priorities in health care. The silver lining is that resource scarcity has compelled us to evolve a highly leveraged model for facilitating otherwise very labor-intensive critical reflection.

Through this book on discovery, engagement, and leverage, I am now seeking to expand my audience beyond healthcare. I have shared the details of my healthcare program in the hopes that it might stimulate ideas and opportunities for improvement among other professionals. To further facilitate this, I would like to offer a generalized recipe for designing and delivering a leveraged program of client-centered care in other professions. Then I will offer another case study from a different industry, to illustrate the portability and power of my leveraged model of care.

Designing for leverage: the recipe

My experience developing a patient support program has led me to articulate a new approach to program design. I call it designing for leverage. This approach combines elements of user-centered design with discovery-driven planning, agile product development, and public health program design. The specific design elements include: strategic direction; delivery plan; operational plan; evaluation plan; and financial plan. I will now illustrate these design elements while referring to my patient support program, now known as the Patient Support Corps.

The five components of this approach are interlocking. Picture the Olympic rings but so that each one interlocks with all the others. You need to work on all five simultaneously and keep them in constant view as you design and implement a program of client-centered care.

You should be able to summarize your program elements on a single page at all times. You will need to be revising them continually.

The intersection of all five elements forms a star in the diagram below, and that star represents to me the focus of my attention and efforts as the program leader. It's something very small and focused that emerges from five larger components.

The first ring is your strategic direction. This typically includes what strategic planners refer to as vision, purpose, and mission statements along with core values. These have gotten a bad rap because every organization now has them, and they are often anodyne, and they get posted in elevators and ridiculed. I think they are bad mostly when you see them in organizations that really don't have a strategic direction, but think it's important to act as if they did. When organizations do have a strategic direction, short statements summarizing it are orienting and mobilizing for people inside and outside the enterprise.

A vision statement presents the state of the world we are trying to create. Our enduring purpose is how we contribute to that vision. Our current mission is our drive to overcome the most significant barriers to pursuing our purpose.

For the Patient Support Corps, I'm happy to say we do have a strategic direction, and it's easy to articulate. Our vision is a world in which patients are fully informed and involved in making treatment decisions. Our purpose is to provide patients with the support they need to become informed and involved. And our mission is to train students to provide this support. Our core values include a commitment to patient autonomy and self-determination, valid information, and well-considered preferences.

This strategic direction guides all of our activities. Consistent with discovery-driven planning and agile product development, we don't over-specify our plans. We march in the direction of our goals.

The second ring is the product or service delivery plan. This starts with a user-centered map of the client journey, such as the maps I presented above of the patient journey through our clinic. Then we design touch-points for maximum leverage. In the case of the Patient Support Corps, as long as health care is delivered via office visits (a state of affairs tied to current reimbursement practices, which are changing), we expect to touch patients between diagnosis and first specialty care visit, offering materials and services to change their trajectory around decision-making. We are very clear on what materials and services we are delivering. Again, we send patients high quality educational materials and help them list questions, take notes, and make recordings so that they can be more informed and involved in their treatment decisions.

Seeing the patient experience as a journey promotes the right mindset. Here's how Donald Berwick articulated his view of touching the patient journey: "We—patients, families, clinicians, and the health care system as a whole—would all be far better off if we professionals recalibrated our work such that we behaved with patients and families not as hosts in the care system, but as guests in their lives." I fully subscribe to this humble view that places the professional at the service of the patient journey, seeking to fit into it rather than bend the patient experience to fit what is convenient for the professional.

The third ring is the operational plan. This specifies how we marshal and deploy all of our resources to support our service delivery plan. Our operational plan in the Patient Support Corps includes people, infrastructure, supplies, and processes, practices, techniques, and technology. We refer to the operational plan as life support for our service delivery plan. This keeps us mindful of how vital some of our back office activities are to the actual patient experience. If you unplug life support, the patient dies.

This is the one part of our program that is quite complex. Because our staff turns over entirely every year or two, we rely on an operational manual that we keep assiduously up to date. It serves as a reference manual for how we do everything, from scripts for calling patients, to checklists for discovery (SLCT) and engagement (SCOPED).

Our reference manual runs a couple hundred pages of text and screenshots, which we are now migrating to a training platform that will allow us to document our practices in screencasts and videos as well as text. This is a living document that we update every week.

Although our annual turnover creates challenges, in this case it compels us to have very good and constantly updated documentation, which is a benefit. We have found it important to write our documentation as a series of action statements, with a subject, active verb, and object, similar to the best practices in agile product development.

The fourth ring is the evaluation plan. We use the RE-AIM framework to evaluate our program. RE-AIM stands for Reach, Effectiveness, Adoption, Implementation, and Maintenance. Reach means the number or proportion of our target audience that received our products and services; effectiveness is the impact of those offerings; adoption refers to the facilitators and barriers to broader uptake by individuals and organizations who facilitate our service delivery plan; ==implementation== refers to whether our program is delivered with fidelity or adaptations to the intended design; and ==maintenance== refers to whether we are sustaining our impact over time.

We track and refine our performance in all these areas continuously. Many programs measure and try to improve reach and effectiveness. With our attention to adoption, implementation, and maintenance, our hope is that we will stay on top of deeper system dynamics and improve our performance with a much longer horizon in mind.

For example, we have always measured the degree to which we are applying our program capacity to direct service delivery. This is a measure of implementation—of fidelity to our program design. We wanted to make sure that our interns, who had one day per week to work in our program, were getting to serve patients during that day.

In the early days of our program, we found that we were using only 29% of our intern capacity. In other words, for every 10 days on our program, interns were spending only three of them serving patients. When we dug into this, it turned out that we were inefficiently matching interns with patients. We had asked interns to each cover a half-day slot in the clinic. One intern would coach all the patients scheduled for Monday mornings, another would coach those scheduled for Monday afternoons, and so on.

This scheme had the advantage of being convenient for students to anticipate and schedule around. However, the incidence of new patient diagnoses did not follow our professional-centered scheme. From week to week, we saw great variation in demand for any given slot, with some interns unable to keep up with demand and others not finding any patients to serve. So we switched to a more dynamic allocation of program capacity. Every day, our interns call patients with upcoming appointments from a master list, and place interested patients on a waitlist for our services. Each intern then checks the waitlist every day to see if they are available to serve any patient on it. After instituting this change, our exploitation of program capacity increased from 29% to 84%.

This is one of just many examples of how we have continuously improved our program. As the acronym suggests, we are constantly RE-AIMing to adjust our practices and improve our performance. Another key to our success in RE-AIMing the program has been our enlistment of the interns themselves as program redesigners. We meet every week to review cases, and working backwards from these examples of service delivery, we brainstorm opportunities for improvement. Since we don't have time to discuss every case, we use the Critical Incident Technique to review and learn from the most deviant cases—the very best and very worst performances.

Learning from our very worst performances means we have to operate in a culture of mutual learning. No one will freely discuss cases that went very wrong if they think they are going to be blamed or shamed. We use principles and practices from Chris Argyris' Action Science methodology to minimize organizational routines that limit learning. I try to channel Argyris' observation that people who are scientifically minded should approach organizational interactions with the same mindset.

I try to reinforce in every interaction with the interns that we should operate from a place of curiosity, fallibility, and perspective-taking. I contrast this with the encounters we have all had in dysfunctional organizations with leaders and employees who act as control freaks, cover up mistakes, seek to avoid overt conflict, and save face. The most important behavior leaders can model in this regard is always seeking to disconfirm their assumptions, rather than looking for confirmation. Because most people are prone to a social agreement bias, in other words, being agreeable, leaders must bend over backwards to test their assumptions and inferences and look for evidence that they are wrong. Sadly, people generally tell leaders what they think the leaders want to hear, rather than what the leaders need to hear.

The fifth ring in designing for leverage is the financial plan. The key here is to synchronize program revenues and costs in a way that allows you to sustain the delivery of value to clients. This is where professionals often struggle with entitlement. Professionals may have sunk a decade of education and hundreds of thousands of dollars into their training. They have the expectation of earning enough to repay their debts and enjoying a professional standard of living. So they engage in cost-plus budgeting. What does my salary cost, and the other staff, and what are the other costs involved in comfortably delivering our program? There's our budget!

My orientation is that in order to sustain a program, we may need to plan ourselves out of a job. For example, the Patient Support Corps currently operates in an environment where there is relatively little money for patient advocacy or education. I would love to change that environment, but for the foreseeable future I don't see it changing very much. The Patient Support Corps will be much more sustainable when it is student-led, with people like me acting as occasional advisors and consultants instead of directors. The other benefit, of course, will be that student leaders will grow tremendously when given the opportunity to lead.

I've tried to describe designing for leverage with some examples from my program, the Patient Support Corps. I now want to share another case study with you, this one from the world of financial services.

Designing for leverage in financial services

One day, my friend Kevin Hoffberg called with a proposition that I knew would change my life. I met Kevin when I was still at my startup, after finishing my PhD. At the time he was also working for a software company. Kevin had gone on to head marketing in the private client division of Russell Investments, a global multi-asset management company.

On this fateful day, Kevin said something to the effect of, "Jeff, I've been following your work with patients for years. The light bulb went on in my head last night. We should translate your work in healthcare to financial services."

To this end, Kevin and his colleagues at Russell Investments introduced me to Halbert Hargrove Global Advisors (HHGA), a registered investment advisor and certified fiduciary. HHGA is very successful and has been for decades. Russ Hill, HHGA's Chairman, subscribes to Andy Grove's dictum that only the paranoid survive, and he is always looking for a way to improve. Russ and other firm leaders attended one of my presentations, and volunteered HHGA as an early adopter. We started with the SLCT discovery process. I've described some of our work in Chapter 5.

I want to describe in more detail how we applied my designing for leverage approach at HHGA. My hope is that another case study, in a different domain than the last, will help you understand the power of designing leveraged ways for delivering client-centered care.

We implemented designing for leverage after our pilot study with six advisors. That study showed that SLCT was associated with increased advisory inquiry, increased client disclosure, and improved ratings of discovery interviews with clients. Now Russ Hill and his colleagues wanted to expand the program.

Recall that designing for leverage requires constant attention to five domains. First I asked about the client journey. Where might there be some touch points where we could integrate discovery interviews and materially improve the client trajectory?

We went over the archetypal client journey. Someone comes to understand, often through a significant event in their family, that they are being either undertreated or over-treated when it comes to advice about their wealth. The significant event may be marriage, divorce, children, saving for college, retirement, illness, or death.

A center of influence (such as another professional, e.g. estate planner, or an existing client) refers the prospective client to HHGA; or the prospective client finds HHGA online and self-refers.

A regional director at HHGA then speaks with the prospective client and determines whether there is a good fit. HHGA has certain eligibility criteria for their prospective clients, including a minimum amount to open an account; an orientation toward disciplined, long-term, diversified investing; and complex needs that warrant HHGA's full-service approach to wealth advice.

Assuming there is a fit, the client commits to transferring funds into an HHGA-managed account and begins a formal process. During this process, a client services manager handles logistics (e.g. getting certain documents signed), while a relationship manager reviews the client needs and works with the regional director to construct an investment strategy and make referrals to other professionals formally or informally affiliated with HHGA, for tax or estate planning or other services.

HHGA puts the client on a roadmap laying out the agenda for quarterly meetings at which team members review portfolio performance and client needs and make adjustments. This goes on for years, with certain inflection points when clients and their families again experience major changes such as marriages, divorces, children, saving for college, retirement, illness, and death.

In looking for discovery touchpoints, we identified several potential service delivery scenarios. We could apply SLCT discovery to prospective clients as part of the courtship dance; or to brand new clients during the onboarding process; or to existing clients facing major life changes; or to the uninvolved spouses, often wives, who frequently outlived their husbands and suddenly needed to interact with financial advisors.

We honed in on enhancing discovery during the courtship phase of the client journey. HHGA leaders felt that the potential impact was enormous. Surfacing the full client agenda would allow both parties to determine whether there was really a good fit at a deeper level of understanding. A good fit is a win/win situation that plays out for decades. Conversely, a bad fit is expensive and painful for both parties.

Within the courtship phase of the client journey, there was a specific referral path that HHGA felt bore improving. This was a brokerage referral program. The partner company in question is a large broker that formally refers many of its clients to wealth advisors when the clients feel they need broader services than they can provide. In such cases, the broker refers clients to three or four wealth advisors.

HHGA felt that we could initially focus our enhanced discovery initiative on this program. As described in Chapter 5, we documented a 22% close rate for advisors before training.

Having identified where we felt we could most productively enhance the client journey, we articulated our strategic direction for this new program as follows.

Strategic Direction

- The purpose of the referral response program is to entice desirable referrals to entrust their assets to HHGA.
- The vision or desired end-state is a world in which the broker thinks of HHGA first when making referrals because referred clients are so delighted with HHGA's response.
- The short-term mission is to increase the close rate from current levels of 22%. This is a close rate of between one in four and one in five. As a matter of policy, the broker refers their clients to three or four advisors. Therefore a close rate of one in four is to be expected if HHGA is competitive but not differentiated. Our short-term mission is to increase the close rate to one in three in responding to the broker referrals.

- The strategic approach is to transition HHGA from an individual proposal to a team-based discovery approach to responding to referrals.

The last element of our strategic direction referred to our proposed innovations in the service delivery and operational plans.

Regarding the service delivery plan: previously each regional director was solely responsible for fielding and responding to broker referrals. Regional directors usually met prospective clients in person and conducted discovery interviews rather informally with very little documentation. From HHGA's perspective, it was difficult to monitor, measure, and improve upon this informal process, which reflected tremendous individual variation depending on the regional director's personality and working style.

We now decided to modify the service delivery plan so that prospective clients would meet by telephone with the client services manager, relationship manager, and regional director all at once. One of the junior members of the team (either the client services manager or relationship manager) would administer the SLCT discovery process and create a discovery note. If the client appeared to be a good fit with HHGA, and was interested in proceeding, the HHGA entire team would then meet to prepare a response that addressed the documented client needs point by point. Finally, the team would get back on the telephone with the client and present the response.

This service delivery plan clearly had implications for the operational plan. The idea was for client services managers and relationship managers, who are based at HHGA headquarters, to take on more of the discovery and response tasks. They could assure more structured documentation in the firm's new customer relationship management system. HHGA wanted their field representatives, the regional directors, to spend more time out in the field securing additional referrals from other centers of influence.

Our thinking was that regional directors could do this if client services managers and relationship managers were shouldering more of the work of discovery and response to existing referrals. This kind of task shifting is common when re-engineering a service delivery plan. In medicine the expression is that we want "everyone practicing at the top of their license." Now, talented and well-trained client services managers would exceed their prior focus on more clerical tasks, which they could delegate to interns or administrative assistants.

The only other major operational change was that we made greater use than ever before of HHGA's teleconferencing system, and recorded all the client calls for training and quality improvement purposes. Whereas previously the regional director discovery and response practices were unknown and unknowable, now HHGA can review all discovery and response meetings conducted with prospective clients.

Our evaluation plan followed the RE-AIM framework. Our target for reach was to respond promptly to all of the prospective clients referred by the broker. Our primary measure of effectiveness was close rate.

We were interested in facilitators or barriers to adoption, especially among regional directors, whom we were asking to move from an individually-based sales model to a team-based sales model.

According to Rogers' Diffusion of Innovations theory, five factors facilitate adoption. Other than relative advantage (captured in close rate, above), these consist of trialability; simplicity; observability; and compatibility. We monitored our program with these in mind.

We made sure that participants knew our trial would be reversed if it was not working out. We made sure that team experiences were observable to other teams, as we reviewed cases regularly across teams; and we monitored whether the SLCT process was simple enough to be feasible for both advisor teams and prospective clients. We quickly established that these adoption factors were in our favor. A more complicated question was whether the team-based approach would be compatible with the regional director workstyle, and compatible with client services manager and relationship manager workloads.

We addressed this in our evaluation of implementation fidelity and adaptations. We felt it was vital that regional directors adhere with high fidelity to our program design. This was initially a challenge because the regional directors continued to field referrals directly from the broker, rather than sharing them with the team. By force of habit, they tended to initiate at least one call with prospective clients before setting up the team-based conference call.

That one call represented a vestige of individually-driven practice, since inevitably they would get into conversations that went relatively undocumented as before. Our project Steering Committee convinced the regional directors to adhere to our design and soon they were setting up team-based conference calls as requested.

We quickly documented early successes with the team-based administration of SLCT, which was associated with 58% close rates, compared with 22% beforehand. Our last element of RE-AIM evaluation is maintenance. It is too soon to tell, but we will eventually know whether the positive impact of SLCT discovery is maintained, from outcomes such as client retention, increase in assets under management, satisfaction, and referrals.

Finally, we developed a financial plan for this enhanced discovery program. HHGA considers the details to be trade secrets, but suffice it to say that their estimates show that the projected revenues vastly exceed the projected costs, which include my professional fees for consulting, training, and coaching.

I have been delighted to validate my approach to designing for leverage in a completely different environment than that of the Patient Support Corps. I have since initiated other projects in financial services and although it's too early for definitive findings, early results are equally promising.

After working on this puzzle of discovery, engagement, and leverage for twenty years, I am happy to offer my insights and lessons learned to the world. I wrote this book to leverage my own efforts, so that professionals can read it and self-administer any of my prescriptions. Inevitably, there will be limits to how far readers can implement their own leveraged programs for discovery and engagement. In the next chapter, I offer some thoughts on how I may be of further assistance to individuals and organizations wishing to pursue more client-centered care.

Chapter 7 concept map

Designing for leverage begins with establishing a strategic direction. This includes expressing the vision or desired state of the world that a program should achieve; the program's long-term purpose in moving the world in the direction of the vision; and the short-term mission that compels immediate action. Ideally you will articulate the strategic direction in completely client-centered terms. With this strategic direction to guide you, you should next map the client journey and corresponding program touchpoints. This will become your service delivery plan. You will then design your operational plan to support your delivery of services, and a financial plan to ensure that revenues and costs are synchronized for maximum sustainability. All the while, you will evaluate your program's reach, effectiveness, adoption, implementation, and maintenance.

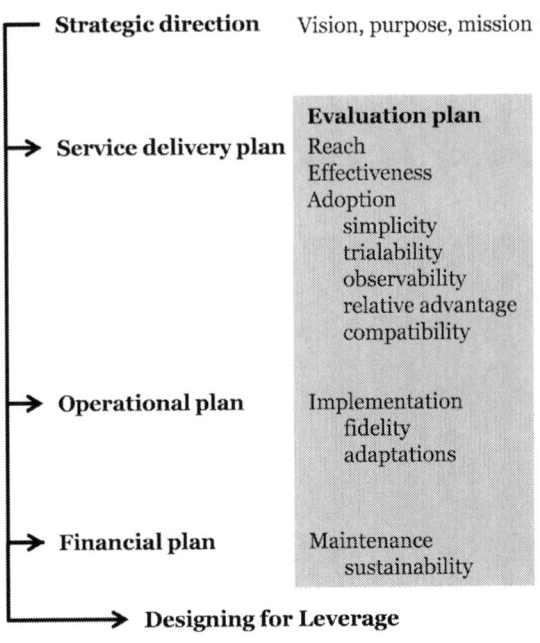

Strategic direction — Vision, purpose, mission

Service delivery plan — **Evaluation plan**
Reach
Effectiveness
Adoption
   simplicity
   trialability
   observability
   relative advantage
   compatibility

Operational plan — Implementation
   fidelity
   adaptations

Financial plan — Maintenance
   sustainability

→ **Designing for Leverage**

DEAL! Recipes: Chapter 8

Let's make a DEAL!

Never doubt that a small group of thoughtful, committed citizens can change the world. Indeed, it is the only thing that ever has.

Margaret Meade

I've covered a lot of territory in the chapters above: five life drivers, four strategies for critical reflection, the FAST process for critical reflection, the SLCT discovery process, the SCOPED decision process, and a leveraged approach to program design. These tools amount to a new DEAL for professionals: new tools for discovery, engagement, and leverage.

In my own personal and professional life, I use these approaches separately and together. As an individual contributor in an organization, you should be able to take on these frameworks one at a time and implement them to some good effect.

More ambitious is to implement them in an integrated fashion. In Chapter 7, on leverage, I described my own patient support program as a case study, and my work with a financial services firm applying my designing for leverage approach to program design.

In case you need further assistance to adopt and implement parts or all of my new DEAL, I'd like to describe some of my additional offerings. While this book will enable some professionals to self-administer everything they need to implement the DEAL framework, many of you will desire further assistance. I offer a range of services to help motivated and resourceful organizations translate DEAL into practice.

Designing for leverage consultations

As much as I believe in the transformative power of training, it's a big ask for professionals to attend brief training and then transform their practices. If you want to conduct training in your organization at any scale, and you expect transformed practices and improved outcomes, you need a well-designed, comprehensive implementation program.

However, as I mentioned earlier, I'm not a fan of over-specified programs. The most realistic programs are adaptive in that they plan for flexibility. Also, I am suspicious of programs that proceed with cost-plus budgeting and generally increase (or maintain) the existing cost of delivering services.

That's why I developed my five-step approach to program design, described in Chapter 7, and called it designing for leverage. This approach is inspired by and consistent with discovery-driven planning and its offshoots, agile and adaptive product design. I consult with internal champions throughout the process of articulating the strategic direction; mapping the client journey and service delivery plan; leveraging the human and other resources needed to touch the client at key points on their journey; synchronizing costs and revenues for financial sustainability; and evaluating the program. This should result in a program that is pragmatic and delivers high returns to clients and professionals alike.

Experiential Learning/Stepwise Training Curriculum

Once we have a program outlined, training is the main way I can help you implement my new DEAL. For each of the tools or techniques we have covered in this book, I have developed an Experiential Learning/Stepwise Training Curriculum (ELSTC, pronounced "elastic.") I will now share the outlines of this curriculum in case you want a preview or would like to adapt and implement it yourself.

Over the course of conducting my first 88 workshops on this material, I evolved this curriculum to be maximally engaging and effective. Recently I've found it works equally well online as in person. Either way, the training has to be experiential. In order to be experiential, I need learners to bring personal case studies to our sessions.

Specifically, I ask learners to write two case studies before registering. The case studies should be de-identified to protect privacy, and can be fictionalized, but should be based on personal experience.

For example, when teaching SLCT discovery in health care, I ask students to prepare cases about patients facing treatment decisions and getting ready to consult a physician. Each case consists of a paragraph summarizing the patient diagnosis and treatment options, as well as an initial list of questions and concerns. Learners can draw on their direct experience with their own health; or their indirect experience with family members. Here's an example submitted by a learner recently:

> Fred is a 65-year-old, recently divorced man, currently living on his own. As a retired news reporter, Fred makes a meager income. He has been diagnosed with gastric cancer, but by the time it was found, the cancer had spread irrevocably. After operating, his surgeon informed Fred that he had three to six months left to live. Fred is about to visit his oncologist in order to discuss his treatment options. The doctor has talked about chemotherapy, but estimates the chance of survival past six months is around 20% along with potentially severe health impacts during treatment. Having just welcomed a new grand-daughter into the world, Fred is deciding between this exhaustive

chemotherapy or simply going without treatment.

For the same SLCT discovery training in financial services, I might request a personal case about an investor facing retirement who is interviewing financial advisors. A recent case submitted by a learner in financial services was:

> Terry is a prospective client who says, "I've worked hard for a very long time to get to a reasonably comfortable position. And obviously, being sufficiently defensive to protect that is a high priority. I don't have huge inheritance ambitions, you know, our kids are pretty much standing on their own, and we only have one grandchild, so that's not an issue. I have a school that I'd really like to support because it's made all the difference in my life." He thinks he will predecease his wife and wants her to be able to work effectively with his advisory firm. He is very pleased with her increasing engagement in their financial affairs.

My point in showing these diverse personal cases is that the examples used for learning reflect the particular domain—whether health care or financial services or any other industry.

With the development of these brief personal cases, my learners put themselves in their client's shoes when participating in my workshop. They are ready to interpret all of the concepts and training through the filter of a specific client. I want my learners to be thinking, "How would this work for the client in *my* case?"

The next step in the curriculum is that my learners conduct a baseline interaction with a simulated client. Their assignment is to attempt to perform the task they will be learning from me.

So, in my SLCT discovery workshop, I ask learners to conduct a discovery interview as they would right now, before training. In my SCOPED decision workshop, learners must help their simulated client make a decision, before learning SCOPED.

Either I supply simulated clients, or the learners pair up and use their personal cases to role-play clients for one another. Each learner audio-records their client interaction and transcribes it, so as better to absorb their pre-training practices. Then they reflect on their performance and create learning goals for the upcoming training. Again this primes my learners to receive instruction. They become acutely aware of their strengths at baseline—and also their opportunities for improvement.

Next my learners review a full speed demonstration. For example, I might show them or demonstrate a SLCT discovery or SCOPED interview with a real or simulated client. This provides them with an idealized picture of what they will learn. It becomes a target for learning.

At last we are ready for instruction in the new skill. Learners review a slow motion demonstration in which I break down the new skill into progressive steps. I teach them how to do a single step; and then the learners practice that single step with a simulated client. Once the learner has mastered that step, he or she moves on to the next.

The final assignment is for the learners to conduct a full speed interaction with a simulated client in which they perform the new skill. This is the same assignment as the baseline simulation. This time, however, the learner is practicing newly learned techniques. Again the learner must record and transcribe their interaction and obtain instructor feedback.

Learners repeat this final assignment until they have demonstrated proficiency. My training is all about developing new cognitive and interpersonal skills. There is no didactic instruction, no reading, and no slides. I call it a stepwise curriculum because it brings learners through a progression of modules that each builds on the previous. I keep close tabs on feedback from my learners and I'm happy to report the curriculum is extremely highly rated.

For example, in the first half of 2015, I conducted six SCOPED workshops attended by 1,076 learners in group sizes ranging from 55 to 315. Of these, 932 audience members (87%) filled out and turned in an evaluation survey. I developed this workshop based on years of feedback from similar surveys, so I was confident that it would work well, but ongoing feedback allows me to continuously improve.

The quantitative results were as follows. On a scale of 1 (poor) to 5 (excellent), 912 respondents rated the workshop as 3 (good), 4 (very good) or 5 (excellent). In other words, all but 21 learners out of 1,076 gave it positive ratings. Almost half of the respondents (390 or 42%) rated the workshop as 5/5.

My survey also asked the learners to compare the workshop to other sessions they've attended in the last year. Almost two-thirds of the respondents rated it "better" (64%); only 4% rated it "worse."

As outlined in previous chapters, researchers have documented client benefits from implementing SLCT and SCOPED with a well-trained workforce. In health care, patients have reported reductions in anxiety, distress, decisional conflict, and regret; and increases in satisfaction, self-efficacy, knowledge, and decision quality. In financial services, we are beginning to see increased client disclosure, satisfaction, and close rates, and we are monitoring longer term outcomes as well.

Online training

I've been pleasantly surprised by recent developments in online training. Many online courses consist of watching videos and taking quizzes. Nothing inherently wrong with that, but it's totally inadequate for my Experiential Learning/Stepwise Training Curriculum. This curriculum relies heavily on learners interacting with others and getting individualized feedback from instructors or coaches.

Recently, though, I've found online learning management systems that deliver my curriculum in ways that may exceed in-person training. Using my online platforms, I can enroll learners anywhere, any time. They submit their assignments electronically, starting with their personal case studies. Next, they upload recordings, transcripts, and reflections related to their baseline interactions with simulated clients. They follow along as I demonstrate, via screencast, the skills they are learning. Then they review stepwise modules to learn and practice each of the building blocks that comprise their new skill. Finally, they upload recordings, transcripts, and reflections of their post-training interactions with simulated clients. All along the way, I provide feedback, or if I'm not available, I deputize one of my experienced colleagues to respond to the next assignment in the queue.

The secret is that the online training is really hybrid training. The instruction takes place online. However, the learner practices with simulated clients in person or by telephone. As long as they capture a recording and transcribe it, my colleagues and I can review it and give feedback.

What is good about online training is that instructors can give more individualized feedback. When I'm running an Experiential Learning/Stepwise Training workshop in person, we have quiet or shy learners alongside extroverts. Inevitably the extroverts ask more questions and get more feedback. Also, we are engaged in synchronous communication, and when time expires, it's time to move on. Online, my learners can take all the time they need to absorb lessons, and all the time they need to formulate and ask me questions. I can take all the time I need to respond.

I'm actively moving all my workshops online so that I can respond to client needs for in person or online training equally well.

Coaching

I believe coaching is a key ingredient in any leveraged program design. Coaches can implement commitment strategies and act as accountability partners in ways that help learners master new skills.

I have done a lot of coaching as part of training, supervising, and mentoring new learners. However, in a leveraged program to implement my new DEAL, we will probably find more cost-effective coaches.

You will want to reserve me for high level coaching, which amounts to the design consultations I've described above. We can recruit and train practice-related coaches from other sources.

As you may recall, one of my mantras from health care is "everyone practicing at the top of their license." In my experience, junior people, recently trained and new to the field, often make outstanding coaches. They are usually unencumbered with dysfunctional practices. They can hold others accountable to enacting a new skill with high fidelity.

Some senior professionals will resist being coached by their juniors. In fact, we are selecting junior coaches precisely because they are less experienced. Very junior coaches following a client-centered protocol can often help senior professionals overcome professional-centered habits, such as use of jargon. Junior coaches usually haven't had time to develop as many professional-centered habits.

Speaking

I am always happy to serve audiences from the stage. Often my hosts want me to motivate and entertain while audiences sit back and enjoy the show. This can be an appropriate way of stimulating professionals to think different, as Steve Jobs would say.

My best innovation in this area, however, is something I call the keynote workshop. I've found the best way to transfer skills to an audience is to engage them in experiential learning. This is possible even with very large audiences. I've delivered somewhat abbreviated versions of my Experiential Learning/Stepwise Training curriculum to audiences as large as 450, and I don't think there is any real upper limit.

The key is to assign individual and paired exercises. Even in very large auditoriums, audience members can always think, talk, read, and write. They can do three of these things quietly, and turn to their neighbors when it's time to talk.

I generally motivate the topic at hand (e.g. decision-making) with a dramatic opening story. Then I assign audience members to develop a brief personal case study on the spot. This is an individual written exercise.

Next I'll ask audience members to pair up and attempt a baseline application of their skill (e.g. help your neighbor reflect critically on an upcoming decision.)

I'll ask for comments and questions, and then demonstrate how I would apply the skill in question (e.g. SCOPED), often with a volunteer from the audience. People pay close attention when I go live with a volunteer. Who knows what might happen?

I will conduct my full-speed demonstration, then invite the audience members to pair up and practice their new skill. If there's time, first we'll do some slow motion skill building. Otherwise the audience just jumps in the deep end and swims.

The keynote workshop has become my favorite mode of presentation, probably because it stretches me to my capacity as a teacher and stage performer, and reaches so many people live.

The key requirement for success is to manage audience expectations in advance. An audience settling in to a large auditorium sometimes feels it has earned the right to be passive. A few audience members will therefore resist being called into action if that was not their expectation.

With the right advance communication and expectation setting, however, I've found that audiences love my keynote workshops. Sadly, many professionals have only experienced didactic training:

long, droning slide presentations. Most have never experienced anything as interactive and effective as my Experiential Learning/Stepwise Training curriculum, even in a small workshop. Then they are surprised to find that they can be active learners even while sitting in a large auditorium!

In summary, if you want to expose a large group to my new DEAL, I will be there for you in whatever format works best for your audience. I just hope you will consider the keynote workshop in addition to more conventional formats.

My approach to intellectual property

My mission is to help professionals guide clients to good decisions. I sustain this mission through commercial offerings that subsidize my ongoing research and development. These offerings also subsidize my passion for working in underfunded areas such as patient advocacy.

Anyone in my position must strike a balance between giving everything away for free versus holding on so tightly that nothing spreads. My approach is to charge royalties for licenses to my copyrighted materials; fees for consulting services; and honoraria for speaking. May we all prosper together.

In conclusion

I have spent more than 20 years figuring out how to guide people to good decisions. I have had tremendous support along the way, and the acknowledgments section of this book is devoted to highlighting the mentorship, collaboration, and investments of many others. It's a pleasure to share with you the fruits of my labors. It's taken a long time to get to a point of sufficient simplicity that I could expect broad adoption of my techniques.

In essence, throughout this book, I propose that four strategies of critical reflection will enhance three domains of decision quality. The four strategies are thinking, talking, reading, and writing. The three domains of decision quality are clarity, serenity, and harmony. This is the central message of this book: improving decision quality through enhanced critical reflection. You can improve critical reflection on several levels. You can start with better balance among the four strategies of thinking, talking, reading, and writing. You can progress to sequencing your critical reflection using the FAST process: formulate, analyze, synthesize, and translate. Finally, you can help your clients formulate their agenda using SLCT and analyze issues, synthesize insights, and translate insights into action using SCOPED. You can accomplish all this by leveraging junior people in your workforce so everyone is practicing at the top of their license.

In closing, to paraphrase T.S. Eliot, now that we are done with all our exploring, we have arrived where we started: your clients turning to you for guidance in a crisis. You now have powerful new tools to guide your clients to better decisions.

Chapter 8 concept map

Some professionals will be able to implement discovery, engagement, and leverage on their own after reading this book. For those who desire my assistance, I recommend beginning with a program design consultation, followed by training in SLCT and SCOPED. We can usually arrange for cost-effective peer coaching and support. Finally, as a speaker, I can articulate the need for better discovery, engagement, and leverage; or engage even very large audiences in a keynote workshop to teach any of the DEAL ingredients.

Translating *DEAL!* into practice

→ **Consulting** Design for leverage

→ **Training** SLCT discovery
SCOPED decision support
Experiential learning
In-person or online

→ **Speaking** Keynote workshop

→ **Coaching** Peer support

Executive Summary

Not that the story need be long, but it will take a long while to make it short.

> Henry David Thoreau

DEAL! teaches professionals how to guide your clients to good decisions. You'll know that your clients are making better decisions when they act with greater clarity, serenity, and harmony. Clarity is knowing what to do. Serenity is the confidence that comes with having chosen wisely. Harmony is the support and resources needed to act decisively. Conversely, clients make bad decisions when they are confused, anxious, and conflicted.

You can help your clients feel clear, serene, and harmonious by helping them reflect critically on their decisions. Critical reflection means thinking, talking, reading, and writing. Here is a concept map of my key message:

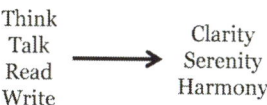

This is the heart of my teaching. You can use these strategies—thinking, talking, reading, and writing—to produce these client benefits: clarity, serenity, and harmony. Let me show you how.

Section 1 Summary

Chapter 1: Five Life Drivers. Five drivers compel your clients to action: somatic, social, spiritual, soulful, and scientific. Somatic refers to the limbic system, instincts, reflexes, emotions. Social refers to people and institutions that influence us. Spiritual refers to how we seek guidance from a higher power. Soulful refers to how we rely on introspection, identity, self-image and conscience. Scientific refers to how we rationally deliberate and analyze. Many of these drivers operate on your clients at a subconscious level.

Somatic, Social, Spiritual, Soulful, Scientific
↓
Decisions

Chapter 2: Decision Quality. Ideally, your clients experience clarity, serenity, and harmony as they act on the five life drivers. Clarity is knowing what to do. Serenity is the confidence that comes with having chosen wisely. Harmony is the support and resources needed to act decisively. Often, however, your clients come to you because they are experiencing whiplash: confusion, anxiety, and conflict. This whiplash is usually the result of mixed signals from the five drivers described above.

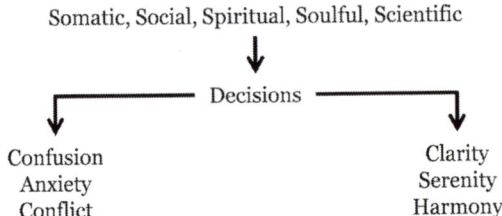

Chapter 3: Strategies for Critical Reflection. To guide your clients in such times of crisis or opportunity, you can help them reflect critically. This simply means thinking, talking, reading, and writing. Your clients will generally have thought and talked more than they will have read and written. Often, just helping them to reflect critically in a more balanced manner will lead to improved clarity, serenity, and harmony.

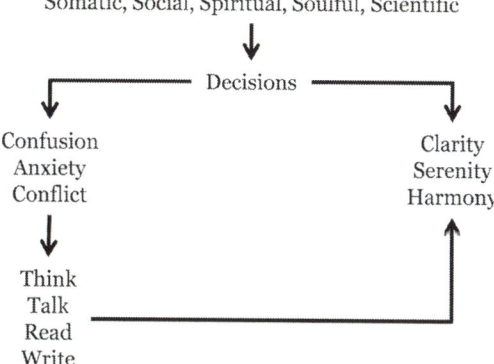

Chapter 4: FAST Critical Reflection. My overall prescription for thinking, talking, reading, and writing with clients is as follows:
1. Formulate the client agenda and document all the issues;
2. Analyze the issues raised by the client;
3. Synthesize insights;
4. Translate insights into action.

Some professionals will improvise their own specific methods for implementing the FAST process for client-centered care. Others will want more specific guidance, which I present in Section 2. Either way, you can use FAST to sequence critical reflection with your clients for maximum effectiveness.

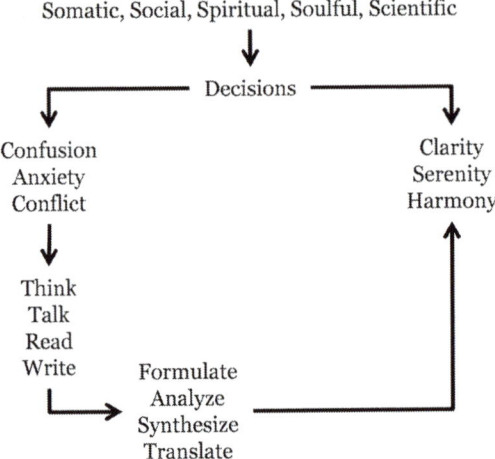

Section 2 Summary

Chapter 5: Discovery. To formulate the client agenda, you need to conduct discovery interviews. I developed a discovery interview protocol that has been associated with increased client disclosure in health care and financial services. It consists of scribing (documenting an initial list of issues without interrupting); laddering (prompting the client to elaborate); checking (administering a checklist to stimulate broader disclosure); and triaging (editing for brevity). The steps spell SLCT, pronounced "select." I present specific instructions and detailed examples so that you too can conduct SLCT discovery interviews with your clients.

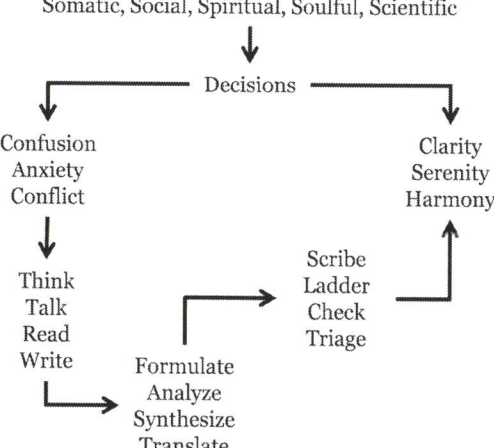

Chapter 6: Engagement. To analyze issues, synthesize insights, and translate insights into action, you need to engage in decision support with your clients. I developed a decision support protocol that has been associated with improved decision quality in medicine. This protocol consists of listing the following:
1. known facts about the situation;
2. available choices;
3. key objectives;
4. roles and responsibilities of people involved or affected by the decision;
5. your evaluation regarding the impact of the choices;
6. and your decision regarding the best choice and next steps.

The first letters of the key words above spell SCOPED: situation, choices, objectives, people, evaluation, decisions. I present specific instructions and detailed examples so that you too can SCOPE client decisions.

Now my concept map for *DEAL!* shows, with a dotted line, that you can use SLCT to formulate the client agenda and SCOPED to analyze, synthesize, and translate it into action:

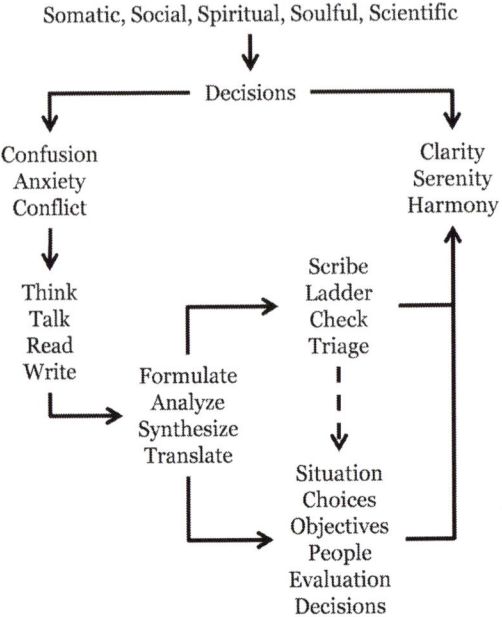

Chapter 7: Leverage. The FAST process generally, and SLCT and SCOPED more specifically, are labor-intensive protocols. To implement them cost-effectively, you must design a program tailored to the client journey and that leverages your organizational resources. I present an approach to program design called designing for leverage. A key feature of this approach is task-shifting so that everyone is practicing at the top of their license. For example, trainees or other very junior members of the workforce are ideally suited to administer early iterations of SLCT and SCOPED, which more senior colleagues can then refine.

More generally, designing for leverage consists of five interlocking parts: strategic direction; service delivery plan; operational plan; financial plan; and evaluation plan. Ideally you will express your strategic direction in client-centered terms, then map the client journey and support it through an efficient service delivery plan. This in turn relies on articulating an operational plan for deploying resources efficiently, which requires a financial plan that synchronizes costs and revenues. Finally, the evaluation plan cuts across all activities. In evaluating your program, you will continuously monitor and improve its reach, effectiveness, adoption, implementation, and maintenance.

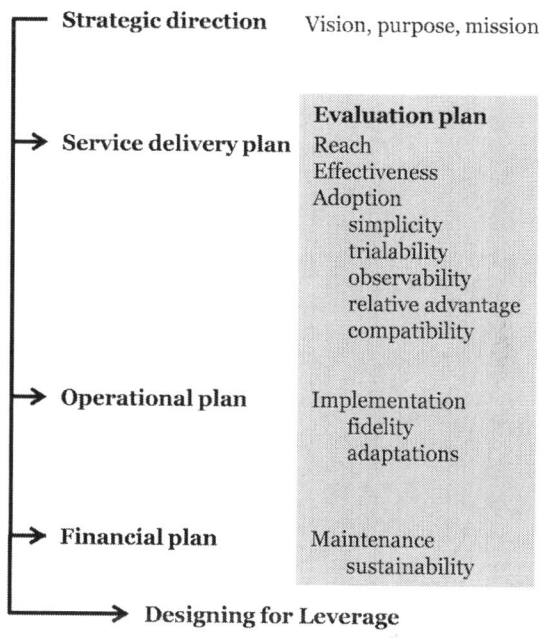

Chapter 8: Let's Make a DEAL! Some organizations will be able to implement discovery, engagement, and leverage on their own after reading this book. For those desiring more assistance, I am available for consulting, training, and speaking. As a consultant, I can help organizations with program design and evaluation. As a trainer, I deliver experiential learning online or in-person. As a speaker, I am known for my keynote workshops to very large audiences, wherein I also emphasize experiential learning.

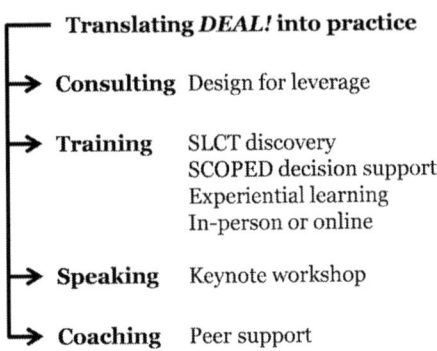

- **Translating *DEAL!* into practice**
- **Consulting** — Design for leverage
- **Training** — SLCT discovery
  SCOPED decision support
  Experiential learning
  In-person or online
- **Speaking** — Keynote workshop
- **Coaching** — Peer support

Bibliography

Books serve to show a man that those original thoughts of his aren't very new after all.

Abraham Lincoln

Additional Sources

You can find additional references relevant to my development of DEAL at the following website links:

www.jeffbelkora.com/evidence, where I list my peer-reviewed journal articles, as well as relevant studies by other researchers;

www.jeffbelkora.com/good-books, where I list books that have influenced my work in general terms.

Below I cite some key references relevant to the specific content of each chapter in turn. I only cite a reference once, in the earliest chapter to which it is relevant.

Target Audience

Breu, Giovanna. "Vision Quest." People, April 3 2000. www.people.com/people/archive/article/0,,20130870,00.html.

Bernard Shaw, George. The Doctor's Dilemma, with Preface on Doctors. New York: Brentano's, 1913.

Christensen, Clayton M. The Innovator's Dilemma: When New Technologies Cause Great Firms to Fail. Boston, MA: Harvard Business School Press, 1997.

Institute of Medicine. Committee on Quality of Health Care in America. Crossing the Quality Chasm: A New Health System for the 21st Century. Washington, DC: National Academy Press, 2001.

Wilson, Timothy D. Strangers to Ourselves: Discovering the Adaptive Unconscious. Cambridge, MA: Belknap Press of Harvard University Press, 2002.

The Story Behind *DEAL!*

You can review a brief description of my patient support program at http://www.jeffbelkora.com/mayo-clinic-video. The Mayo Clinic Center for Innovation recognized our program with an innovation award, and I presented the program with a student intern, Alexandra Teng.

The US Department of Health and Human Services and its Agency for Healthcare Research and Quality cited my patient support program in the following publications:

Agency for Healthcare Research and Quality. "National Healthcare Quality Report." Rockville, MD: U.S. Dept. of Health and Human Services, Agency for Healthcare Research and Quality, 2010. Reviewed on p. 23 under Decision Services. http://archive.ahrq.gov/research/findings/nhqrdr/nhqr10/nhqr10.pdf.

AHRQ Health Care Innovations Exchange. Innovation Profile: Personalized Support Improves Patient-Physician Communication and Enhances Decisionmaking (Jeff Belkora). In: AHRQ Health Care Innovations Exchange [Web site]. Rockville (MD): 2015 09 16. https://innovations.ahrq.gov/profiles/personalized-support-improves-patient-physician-communication-and-enhances-decisionmaking

My colleagues and I recently evaluated the first seven years of our patient support program:

Belkora, J., S. Volz, M. Loth, A. Teng, M. Zarin-Pass, D. Moore, and L. Esserman. "Coaching Patients in the Use of Decision and Communication Aids: Re-Aim Evaluation of a Patient Support Program." BMC Health Serv Res 15, no. 1 (2015): 209. That article is at: http://www.biomedcentral.com/1472-6963/15/209.

Brownlee, Shannon. Overtreated: Why Too Much Medicine Is Making Us Sicker and Poorer. 1st U.S. ed. New York, NY: Bloomsbury, 2007.

Gruman, Jessie C. Aftershock: What to Do When the Doctor Gives You, or Someone You Love, a Devastating Diagnosis. 1st U.S. ed. New York, NY: Walker & Co., 2007.

Hallisy, Julia. The Empowered Patient: Hundreds of Life-Saving Facts, Action Steps and Strategies You Need to Know. San Francisco, CA: Bold Spirit Press, 2008.

Wennberg, John E. Tracking Medicine: A Researcher's Quest to Understand Health Care. New York, NY: Oxford University Press, 2010.

Chapter 1—Five Life Drivers

De Becker, Gavin. The Gift of Fear: Survival Signals That Protect Us from Violence. 1st ed. Boston, MA: Little, Brown, 1997.

Goleman, Daniel. Emotional Intelligence. New York, NY: Bantam Books, 1995.

Gladwell, Malcolm. Blink. New York, NY: Little, Brown, and Company, 2005.

Howard, Ronald A., and Clinton D. Korver. Ethics for the Real World: Creating a Personal Code to Guide Decisions in Work and Life. Boston, MA: Harvard Business Press, 2008.

Kahneman, Daniel. Thinking, Fast and Slow. 1st ed. New York: Farrar, Straus and Giroux, 2011.

Klein, Gary A. Sources of Power: How People Make Decisions. Cambridge, MA: MIT Press, 1998.

Newman, E. A., A. B. Guest, M. A. Helvie, M. A. Roubidoux, A. E. Chang, C. G. Kleer, K. M. Diehl, V. M. Cimmino, L. Pierce, D. Hayes, L. A. Newman, and M. S. Sabel. "Changes in Surgical Management Resulting from Case Review at a Breast Cancer Multidisciplinary Tumor Board." Cancer 107, no. 10 (2006): 2346-51.

Plous, Scott. The Psychology of Judgment and Decision Making, Mcgraw-Hill Series in Social Psychology. New York, NY: McGraw-Hill, 1993.

Robbins, Stephen P. Decide & Conquer: Make Winning Decisions and Take Control of Your Life. Upper Saddle River, NJ: FT Prentice Hall, 2004.

Chapter 2—Decision Quality

Clemen, Robert T. Making Hard Decisions: An Introduction to Decision Analysis. 2nd ed. Belmont, CA: Duxbury Press, 1996.

Csikszentmihalyi, Mihaly. Flow: The Psychology of Optimal Experience. 1st ed. New York, NY: Harper & Row, 1990.

Hammond, John S., Ralph L. Keeney, and Howard Raiffa. Smart Choices: A Practical Guide to Making Better Decisions. Boston, MA: Harvard Business School Press, 1999.

Heath, Chip, and Dan Heath. Decisive: How to Make Better Choices in Life and Work. New York, NY: Crown Business, 2013.

Howard, Ronald A., and Ali E. Abbas. Foundations of Decision Analysis. Upper Saddle River, NJ: Prentice Hall, 2015.

Keeney, Ralph L. Value-Focused Thinking: A Path to Creative Decisionmaking. Cambridge: Harvard University Press, 1992.

Janis, Irving L, and Leon Mann. Decision Making: A Psychological Analysis of Conflict, Choice, and Commitment. New York, NY: The Free Press (Macmillan), 1977.

Matheson, David, and James E. Matheson. The Smart Organization: Creating Value through Strategic R&D. Boston, MA: Harvard Business School Press, 1998.

Chapter 3—Critical Reflection

Aviation Safety Network estimates for 2013 are at http://news.aviation-safety.net/2014/01/01/aviation-safety-network-airliner-accident-fatalities-at-record-low/

Brainwise can be found at www.brainwise-plc.org.

Gawande, Atul. The Checklist Manifesto: How to Get Things Right. 1st ed. New York, NY: Metropolitan Books, 2010.

Gladwell, M. "The Social Life of Paper." New Yorker, March 25, 2002. newyorker.com/magazine/2002/03/25/the-social-life-of-paper.

Kohn, Linda T., Janet Corrigan, and Molla S. Donaldson. To Err Is Human: Building a Safer Health System. Washington, DC: National Academy Press, 2000.

Kondo, M. The Life-Changing Magic of Tidying Up: The Japanese Art of Decluttering and Organizing. Berkeley, CA: Ten Speed Press, 2014.

Rackham, Neil. SPIN Selling. New York, NY: McGraw-Hill, 1988.

Robbins, Stephen P. Decide & Conquer: Make Winning Decisions and Take Control of Your Life. Upper Saddle River, NJ: FT Prentice Hall, 2004.

Chapter 4—FAST Critical Reflection

I maintain a brief description of the FAST process online for quick reference: www.fastprocess.org.

Allen, David. Getting Things Done: The Art of Stress-Free Productivity. New York, NY: Viking, 2001.

Denning, Stephen. The leader's guide to storytelling: mastering the art and discipline of business narrative. San Francisco, CA: Jossey-Bass; 2005.

Doyle, M, D. Straus. How to Make Meetings Work. New York, NY: Jove Books, 1982.

Fried, Jason, David Heinemeier Hansson, and Matthew Linderman. Getting Real: The Smarter, Faster, Easier Way to Build a Successful Web Application. Chicago, IL: 37 signals, 2006.

Kaner, Sam, and Lenny Lind. Facilitator's Guide to Participatory Decision-Making. 2nd ed. San Francisco, CA: John Wiley & Sons/Jossey-Bass, 2007.

Martin, Roger. The Opposable Mind: How Successful Leaders Win through Integrative Thinking. Boston, MA: Harvard Business School Press, 2007.

Schwarz, Roger. The Skilled Facilitator. San Francisco: Jossey-Bass, 1994.

VanGundy, Arthur B. Techniques of Structured Problem Solving. 2nd ed. New York, NY: Van Nostrand Reinhold Co., 1988.

Chapter 5—Discovery

I maintain a brief description of the SLCT process online for quick reference: www.slctprocess.com.

Argyris, Chris. "Action Science and Intervention." Journal of Applied Behavioral Science 19, no. 2 (1983): 115-40.

Beckman, H. B., and R. M. Frankel. "The Effect of Physician Behavior on the Collection of Data." Ann. Intern. Med. 101, no. 5 (1984): 692-6.

Belkora, Jeff. "Evaluating Client Discovery Interviews at a Financial Advisory Firm." Journal of Wealth Management. 18.1 (2015): 9-23. Available online at: www.iinews.com/site/pdfs/JWM_Summer_2015_Belkora.pdf

Belkora, Jeffrey, Melissa Miller, Bonnie Crawford, Kathleen Coyne, Margaret Stauffer, Joanne Buzaglo, Natasha Blakeney, Margo Michaels, and Mitch Golant. "Evaluation of Question-Listing at the Cancer Support Community." Translational Behavioral Medicine 3, no. 2 (2013): 162-71. http://www.ncbi.nlm.nih.gov/pmc/articles/PMC3717975/

Belkora, J. K., A. Teng, S. Volz, M. K. Loth, and L. J. Esserman. "Expanding the Reach of Decision and Communication Aids in a Breast Care Center: A Quality Improvement Study." Patient Educ Couns 83, no. 2 (2011): 234-9.

Belkora, Jeffrey. "Promoting Critical Reflection in Breast Cancer Decision-Making." In Shared Decision-Making in Health Care: Achieving Evidence-Based Patient Choice, edited by Adrian Edwards and Glyn Elwyn, xviii, 414 p. Oxford: Oxford University Press, 2009.

Berger, Warren. A More Beautiful Question: The Power of Inquiry to Spark Breakthrough Ideas. New York, NY: Bloomsbury, 2014.

Brown, R., P. N. Butow, M. J. Boyer, and M. H. Tattersall. "Promoting Patient Participation in the Cancer Consultation: Evaluation of a Prompt Sheet and Coaching in Question-Asking." Br J Cancer 80, no. 1-2 (1999): 242-8.

Butow, P. N., S. M. Dunn, M. H. Tattersall, and Q. J. Jones. "Patient Participation in the Cancer Consultation: Evaluation of a Question Prompt Sheet." Ann Oncol 5, no. 3 (1994): 199-204.

Finder, Robert L. The Financial Professional's Guide to Communication: How to Strengthen Client Relationships and Build New Ones. Upper Saddle River, NJ: Pearson FT Press, 2012.

Kinder, George, and Susan E. Galvan. Lighting the Torch: The Kinder Method of Life Planning. Denver, CO: FPA Press, 2006.

Moore, Steve, and Gary Brooks. Ineffective Habits of Financial Advisors (and the Disciplines to Break Them): A Framework for Avoiding the Mistakes Everyone Else Makes. Hoboken, N.J.: Wiley, 2011.

Noonan, Timothy, and Matthew X. Smith. Someday Rich: Planning for Sustainable Tomorrows Today, Wiley Finance Series. Hoboken, NJ: Wiley, 2012.

Roter, D. L. "Patient Participation in the Patient-Provider Interaction: The Effects of Patient Question Asking on the Quality of Interaction, Satisfaction and Compliance." Health Educ Monogr 5, no. 4 (1977): 281-315.

Rouse, K.R. Putting Money in Its Place. Boston, MA: New England Financial Advisors, 1986.

Chapter 6—Engagement

I maintain a brief description of the SCOPED process at www.scoped.com. There you may download templates and use a web-based app for non-commercial purposes. Contact jeff@jeffbelkora.com to license SCOPED for commercial use.

Pirsig, Robert M. Zen and the Art of Motorcycle Maintenance: An Inquiry into Values. New York, NY: Morrow, 1974.

Piaget, Jean. The Equilibration of Cognitive Structures: The Central Problem of Intellectual Development. Chicago: University of Chicago Press, 1985.

Chapter 7—Leverage

Argyris C, Putnam R, Smith DM: Action Science: Concepts, Methods, and Skills for Research and Intervention. San Francisco, CA: Jossey-Bass; 1985.

Argyris, C. Knowledge for Action: A Guide to Overcoming Barriers to Organizational Change. San Francisco, CA: Jossey-Bass, 1993.

Argyris, Chris. "Teaching Smart People How to Learn." Harvard Business Review, May-June 1991, 99-109.

Belkora, J. K., A. Teng, S. Volz, M. K. Loth, and L. J. Esserman. "Expanding the Reach of Decision and Communication Aids in a Breast Care Center: A Quality Improvement Study." Patient Educ Couns 83, no. 2 (2011): 234-9.

Flanagan, J. C. "The Critical Incident Technique." Psychological Bulletin 51, no. 4 (1954): 327-58.

Collins, James C., and Jerry I. Porras. Built to Last: Successful Habits of Visionary Companies. 1st ed. New York, NY: HarperBusiness, 1994.

Glasgow, R., T. Vogt, and S. Boles. "Evaluating the Public Health Impact of Health Promotion Interventions: The Re-Aim Framework." Am J Public Health 89, no. 9 (1999): 1322-7.

Kinnersley, P., A. Edwards, K. Hood, N. Cadbury, R. Ryan, H. Prout, D. Owen, F. Macbeth, P. Butow, and C. Butler. "Interventions before Consultations for Helping Patients Address Their Information Needs." Cochrane Database Syst Rev, no. 3 (2007): CD004565.

Martin, Roger. The Responsibility Virus. New York, NY: Basic Books, 2002.

Pitkethly, Marie, Stephen MacGillivray, and Rebecca Ryan. "Recordings or Summaries of Consultations for People with Cancer."

Cochrane Database of Systematic Reviews, no. 3 (2008): CD001539.pub2

Rogers, Everett M. Diffusion of Innovations. 5th ed. New York, NY: Free Press, 2003.

Rossi, Peter H., Howard E. Freeman, and Mark W. Lipsey. Evaluation—a Systematic Approach. 6th ed. Thousand Oaks, CA: SAGE Publications, 1999.

Stacey, D., F. Legare, N. F. Col, C. L. Bennett, M. J. Barry, K. B. Eden, M. Holmes-Rovner, H. Llewellyn-Thomas, A. Lyddiatt, R. Thomson, L. Trevena, and J. H. Wu. "Decision Aids for People Facing Health Treatment or Screening Decisions." Cochrane Database Syst Rev 1 (2014): CD001431.

Acknowledgments

This is not the end. It is not even the beginning of the end. But perhaps it is the end of the beginning.

Winston Churchill

I postponed writing *DEAL!* for many years because almost every author laments, in the acknowledgments, the time they had to spend away from their family as they wrote. I'm glad I waited until I could get this done without much disruption to our family life. Every minute with you has been precious, Amy, Ray, and Sky. And thanks to Abbie, Jan, Leila, Randy, Alicia, Noel, Penny, Laurie, and Dave for sharing their love and making our extended family such a joy.

My greatest professional debts of gratitude go to Ron Howard; Laura Esserman; Kevin Hoffberg; and Russ Hill. You are tremendous champions of my personal and professional growth. You have opened doors to major opportunities. Thank you.

I want to use the rest of these acknowledgments to thank the hundreds of collaborators who have also contributed to my development along the way. The easiest way for me to do that is to cluster you by context. Many of you show up in multiple contexts so I will mention you in the context of our first encounter.

I've tried to list all my collaborators, sponsors, supporters, and mentors. I also keep an updated list of organizations that have supported my work at www.jeffbelkora.com/thanks.

First, I'm grateful to the thousands of patients who participated in my research studies at UCSF, Stanford and other sites. Your participation allowed me to ground all my work in the patient experience. You have been my teachers.

Special thanks to my Patient Support Corps colleagues Lauren Stupar, and Shelley Volz; and my UCSF and UC Berkeley intern coordinators over the years: Jennifer Chen, Dan Chen, Meredith Loth, Alexandra Teng, Margot Zarin-Pass, Ekene Obi-Okoye, Jenna Wixon-Genack, Rebecca Small, Lindsay Forbes, Edward Wang, Pete Yeh, and Tia Weinberg. We have shared some truly memorable life lessons.

I'm also grateful to the Breast Care Center student interns who provided services, collected data, made recordings, transcribed case studies, and contributed to continuous improvement in our patient support program. Along with the patients we serve, you have always been the best thing about my day job at UCSF. Thanks to Laura Johnson, Dave Gellis, Laura Petrillo, Christina Minami, Mary Zhang, Theadora Sakata, Juan Lessing, Aprajita Anand, Timothy Hsia, John Parr, Yiwey Shieh, Erin Ebbel, Eugene Fan, Clark Fisher, Andrea Spillmann, Thomas Atwater, James Barnes, Julia Pederson, Hannibal Person, Rajiv Sharma, Amy Heinzerling, Melissa Mueller, Michelle Oboite, Abimbola Orisamolu, Jossy Tseng, June-Ho Kim, Eva Martin, Pamela Tsing, Jessica Bryant, John Connolly, Joyce Lee, Ono Nseyo, Philip Petrou, Erin McCreary, Meredith Bock, Aron Mohan, Jeff Campbell, Aditi Balakrishna, Vickram Tandon, Alexa Glencer, Danny Kim, Adeline Goss, Brittany Harrison, Brandon Perkovich, Matthew Salesi, "Sarah" Yici Zheng, Rebecca Howe, Nilan Schnure, Balim Senman, Alyse Wheelock, Erin Duralde, Kacie Rounds, Hanna Retallack, Kate Serrurier, Mitchell Hayes, Mike Hwang, Booyeon Han, Timothy Henderson, Kelsey Natsuhara, Robin Chin, Karen Tsung, Elizabeth VerHoeve, Annie Wattles, Richard Hwang, Tessa Kaplan, Abhi Jairam, Prihatha Narasimmaraj, Tess O'Meara, Brooke Rice, Dominic Amara, Etienne Gallant, Mamta Shah, Emily Wong, Julia Chambers, Breanna Johnson, April Liang, Patrick Martin-Tuite, Leonie Oostrom, Sarah Rosenberg-Wohl, Hayley Schultz, and Ian Straehley.

Thanks also to the UC Berkeley students who participated in the early iterations of the Patient Support Corps as we refined the model, including: Erika Cagampan, Kevin Chang, Lauren Ciardella, Kaela Connors, Megan Eaves, Jessica Forino, Aliza Goldstein, Saachi

Gupta, Rajika Jindani, Devon Johnson, Mithila Kareti, Chloe Kiester, JJ Kim, Robert Matthews, Joleysa Manese, Chelsie McGirr, Sabrina Marques, Lydia Nelson, Abby Sassaman, Emily Schwab, Margarita Shust, Peng Wang, and Xiteng Yan. Thanks to summer interns Claire Carges, Lucy Deng, Madison Evans, Haley Moulton, Marijoyce Naguit, Anna Young, and Biqi Zhang.

The Informed Medical Decisions Foundation contributed substantial funding to our patient support program for 10 years. For that I am deeply grateful to Meg Bowen, Michael Barry, Jack Fowler, Carrie Levin, Ben Moulton, Al Mulley, Richard Wexler, and colleagues. Thanks also to Don Kemper and colleagues at Healthwise for their leadership in our field of patient engagement. Thanks to Geri Lyn Baumblatt and colleagues at Emmi Solutions for their contributions to the field as well.

The state-funded California Breast Cancer Research Program supported the extension of my work to rural underserved areas in Northern California. On a federal level, I have also had salary support on several large grants at UCSF funded by the Congressionally Directed Medical Research Programs. I am grateful for other salary support over the years from Dartmouth, the Palo Alto Medical Foundation, and the Robert Wood Johnson Foundation. Other salary support included an Independent Research Award from Pfizer and a Bridge Funding award from UCSF.

The Arthur Vining Davis Foundations funded a very early version of my patient support program at UCSF, and recently contributed funding to the establishment of a new chapter of the Patient Support Corps at Dartmouth. Thank you for redoubling your support.

For their current or past financial contributions to the Patient Support Corps, thanks to the Barbara and Gerson Bakar Foundation; the Mount Zion Health Fund; Give Breast Cancer The Boot; the UC Center for Healthcare Quality and Innovation; Jan Farren of US Bank and Pat Armstrong of Wells Fargo and Mario Diaz of the Wells Fargo Foundation; the Miller Foundation; Mr. and Mrs.

Michael Jackson; the Serrurier family; and Gail and Steve Shak. For their donations as well as friendship and moral support, thanks to Alex Panos, Joe Gatto, Tom Chavez, Mary Edlow, Brian Edlow, Trina Weller and Tallis Blalack, Carl Spetzler, Jean Collier-Hurley, Julie and Joe Golden, and Phil Yau and Cynthia Kop.

Thanks also to Ingrid Tauber and the Tauber Family Foundation for supporting the Advanced Breast Cancer Program. At the UCSF Development Office I'd like to thank John Ford, Suzanne Teer, Jody Frederickson and colleagues.

For many years the Patient Support Corps operated entirely within the broader internship program at the UCSF Breast Care Center, where it continues as part of a larger effort today. Thanks to Caryn Aviv, Amy Boebel, Meredith Buxton, Natalie Cox, Sabrina Dias, Kristie Dold, Katherine Forster, and colleagues. This internship program was and continues to be an unparalleled catalyst for innovation.

The Patient Support Corps also depends on the UC Berkeley Undergraduate Research Apprentice Program. Many thanks to Stefanie Ebeling and colleagues.

At a critical time in my career, I benefited from a National Institutes of Health career development award administered at UCSF by Deborah Grady and colleagues. Around the same time, and equally critical to my development, was the UCSF Teaching Scholars Program, thanks to Pat O'Sullivan, Dave Irby, and colleagues.

Since 2008, I have conducted my UCSF research from the Institute for Health Policy Studies and I'm especially grateful to administrators and staff there including Eunice Chee, Stephen Crane, Phyllis Fetto, Lowell Huang, Vince Moulton, Maureen Russo, Jay Sullivan, and Jeannie Wong, among many other esteemed colleagues.

Among many valued collaborators, mentors, and champions at UCSF, I'd especially like to thank Nancy Adler, Michael Alvarado, Nancy Ascher, Alan Ashworth, Paul Asfour, Laurel Bray-Hanin,

Charles Benz, Diana Bretzinger, Mark Bridge, Claire Brindis, Lauren Brown, Peter Carroll, June Chan, Lee-May Chen, Jo Chien, Matt Cooperberg, Elly Cohen, Beth Crawford, Martha Daschbach, Dan Dohan, Charles Dollbaum, Adams Dudley, Suzy Eder, Cheryl Ewing, Elizabeth Fernandez, Emily Finlayson, Rob Foster, Barbara Fowble, Bruce Flynn, Andre Goga, Ron Goldschmidt, Brenda Goldhammer, Ellen Goldstein, Larry Green, Kathy Hajopoulos, Debby Hamolsky, Eve Harris, Sam Hawgood, Bob Hiatt, Jesse Hiatt, Naomi Hoffer, Bethany Hornthal, Katherine Hyland, Michael Kamerick, Stig Kreps, Miriam Kuppermann, Mark Laret, Michelle Melisko, Susan Merrell, BJ Miller, Mark Moasser, Dan Moore, Pam Munster, Laura Olson, Ed O'Neil, Catherine Park, John Park, Rena Pasick, Cynthia Perlis, John Phillips, Steve Polevoi, Michael Potter, Mike Rabow, Hope Rugo, Jason Satterfield, George Sawaya, Hani Sbitany, Sara Schwab, Gerrie Shields, Jon Showstack, Eric Small, Ann Sparkman, Rebecca Sudore, Michael Thomas, Jim Wiley, Leslie Wilson, David Wofsy, Deborah Yano-Fong, and Sue Yom. Thanks to Richard Abbott for permission to record and publish the transcript of our consultation.

Among many valued collaborators and mentors outside of UCSF, my deepest thanks go to Chris Argygris and Karen Sepucha of Harvard University; Carl Spetzler and colleagues at Strategic Decisions Group and the Decision Education Foundation; Phil McArthur, Bob Putnam, and Diana Smith of Action Design; Roger Martin of the University of Toronto; Jill Freidenrich, Ellen Mahoney, and their colleagues at what is now Bay Area Cancer Connections; Nancy Johnson, Mimi Johnson (deceased), Carla Jupiter, Rita Martinez, Sara O'Donnell, and their colleagues at the Cancer Resource Centers of Mendocino County; Paula Cohen of Mendocino Coast Clinics; Russ Hardy of the Ukiah Valley Medical Center; John Rochat of Mendocino Coast District Hospital; Julie Ohnemus and colleagues at the Humboldt Community Breast Health Project; Joanne Buzaglo, Mitch Golant, Kim Thiboldeaux, and colleagues at the Cancer Support Community; Sue Berg, Kathleen Bryar, Nandini

Choudhury, Nan Cochran, Tyler Dillehay, Glyn Elwyn, Elliott Fisher, Ashley Harris, Asha Leichtman, Hilary Llewellyn-Thomas, Martha McDaniel, Elissa Ozanne, Chris Trimble, Dale Collins Vidal, Jim Weinstein, Jack Wennberg, and colleagues at Dartmouth; David Leibowitz, Hal Luft, Cliff Olson, Ming Tai-Seale, Peter Yu, and colleagues at the Palo Alto Medical Foundation; Arnie Milstein, Chip Heath, Doug Owens, Allison Kurian, and colleagues at Stanford University; Mike Hogarth at UC Davis; Victor Montori, David Rosenman and colleagues at the Mayo Clinic; Kevin Bozic and colleagues at the University of Texas; Louise Wallace, Sarah Shepherd, and colleagues at Coventry University; Anna Gregor, Belinda Hacking, Sarah Scott, Elspeth Murray, and colleagues at Edinburgh Cancer Centre; Annette O'Connor, Dawn Stacey and colleagues at the University of Ottawa; Phyllis Butow, Martin Tattersall and colleagues at the University of Sydney, Australia; Ralph Keeney, Gene Washington, Peter Ubel, and colleagues at Duke University; Adrian Edwards at Cardiff University; Clara Lee and colleagues at the University of North Carolina; Kathy Yao and colleagues at Northshore University Health System; Dominick Frosch at the Moore Foundation; Jaime King at UC Hastings; Markus Rumpsfeld at the University of North Norway; Angie Fagerlin, David Hutton, and colleagues at the University of Michigan; Dana Alden at the University of Hawaii; Ricardo Muñoz of Palo Alto University; Marcus Thygeson, Christopher Bogoyevac and colleagues at Blue Shield of California; Janie Zarp and colleagues at Oncology Hematology Consultants; Adam Seifer, Abby Schneiderman, and colleagues at Everplans; Joanna Smith of Healthcare Liaison; Greg Hicks and Rick Foster of FosterHicks; Bill Underwood of Catalyst Consulting Team; Margo Michaels of Health Care Access and Action; Harry and Thelma Saunders of Decision Processes Inc.; Sara Knight of the Veterans Administration; David Latini of Baylor; Debra Roter of Johns Hopkins; Ditka Reiner of Reiner Associates; my executive coaches Marj Plumb and Kendra

Kinnison; Jennifer Brokaw of Good Medicine; Alison Leigh Siegel; Bob Cronin; and Paul Dolan.

Thanks to Russell Investments for launching my career in financial services. It's been a pleasure working with Sandy Cavanaugh, Kevin Hoffberg, Tim Noonan, Michael Winnick and their colleagues including Nate Angelo, Sara Jaenicke, Kristin Gibson, Mollie Jensen, Laurie Marchel, Steve Peterson, Brent Smith, Sam Ushio, and Sarah Weese.

Thanks to the team at Halbert Hargrove Global Advisors, including Russ Hill, JC Abusaid, Kelli Kiemle, Drew Taylor, and colleagues.

I have had the pleasure of working with Mariner Wealth Advisors, including Jana Shoulders, Julie Smith, and colleagues. It's also been an honor to work with Sharon Milligan and colleagues at Wells Fargo Advisors; and with Amy Webber and colleagues at Cambridge Investment Research. Thanks to Ramon Polin for helpful tutorials on the financial services industry.

Thanks to the good people now or formerly at Campuspeak for getting me out on the road in front of audiences: T.J. Sullivan, Amy Butler, David Stollman, Stacey Swift, Andrea Techlin, and colleagues.

Many people launched me on my path before I arrived at UCSF. I'd especially like to thank Ulf Grenander at Brown University; and from Stanford University, Ani Adhikari, John Amos, Hilary Austen, Leslie Berlin, Michael Fehling, Michael Goldbach, Jeannie Kahwajy, Emily Kleeman, Clint Korver, Roberto Ley-Borras, David Lowell, Jim March, Stephanie Mutchnick, Tom Raffin, Miriam Rivera, and David Spiegel.

From my time at Outcome Software, thanks to my colleagues Salman Azhar, Robert Blatt, Jim Gerber, Bruce Dennis, Sandy Erickson, Abdul Rafay Khawaja, Ross Koningstein, Dave Macway, Michelle Mattea, Beverly Powell-Goldman, Allen Stanten, Steve Uhl, Faye van Boxtel, and Jim Walsh.

I'm lucky to have childhood friends who live nearby, including Robert Armas, Cyrus Amini, David King, Marissa Levinson, and Tom Willis. I'm grateful for more recent local friends who also make my days brighter, including Andy Hart, Auren Hoffman, Carlos Monfiglio, Greg Ovalle, Matt Pretzer, and the rest of the guys in Sunday Morning Soccer and Tuesday Morning Hoops. Thanks for keeping in touch from a distance: Amanuel Abate, Stephen Landale Ames, Ali Amiri, Vladimir Douhovnikoff, Yasmin Family, Lee Fox, Mike Furth, Maria Huchberger, Ossi Leikola, Mark Pathmarajah, Jen Pera, and David Rimer. Thanks to Margarita Camarena and Eric Rubin for literally having my back.

Finally, thanks to Guy Kawasaki and Shawn Welch for the useful book *APE: Author, Publisher, Entrepreneur*. I made extensive use of your resources while writing *DEAL!*

Made in the USA
San Bernardino, CA
29 January 2016